What others a
The Inner Ch

An exceptional guideline for not only skaters, but also parents and coaches helping athletes develop their brainpower, control their nerves, and perform at their optimum. The mental toughness techniques cover every situation a skater may face, offering strategies to overcome almost any obstacle.
Edna Chang-Grant: U.S. Figure Skating Parent Committee Chair

An excellent introduction to aspects of mental training and mental skills. Very readable and organized in a good, progressive sequence . . . a valuable contribution.
David Coppel, Ph.D.: Clinical/Sport Psychologist & U.S. Figure Skating Olympic Team Sport Psychologist

A great book for skaters of all levels!
Tammy Gambill: International & National Coach

The most comprehensive and practical guide for the skater's mind! The first edition empowered me through my competitive years. Now with the enhanced second edition, my students and their parents are fully equipped to be part of the next generation of "Inner Champions" on the ice and elsewhere in life.
Beata Handra: U.S. Olympic Team Member

Very well written. . . . I was excited to see that the second edition includes adult skaters. This is a book that will be beneficial to skaters and athletes of ALL ages.
Maggie Harding: U.S. Figure Skating Adult Skating Committee Chair & Adult Gold Ladies II National Champion

Everything I had to do mentally to be successful took me years to learn from sports psychologists. *The Inner Champion* puts all those years into one book.
Dan Hollander: World Competitor & National Medalist

The recipe to become a champion is the combination of a well-developed mind, body, and spirit working as one to achieve the winning edge. The Inner Champion will teach you how to recognize and develop your strengths and eliminate weaknesses in your skating. You will systematically learn how to implement daily mental training techniques essential for reaching your full potential on and off the ice.
     Buddy Lee: Olympian, World Military & U.S. National Wrestling Champion, author of *Jump Rope Training*

A valuable asset. . . . This book provides step-by-step techniques that can help to overcome issues that prevent optimal performance in competition. The Inner Champion is a good read for those skaters who are serious about their sport.
     Tom Lescinski: International & National Coach

The easy-to-understand format allows you to immediately incorporate the various mental skills into your daily training and performance. A "must have" for skaters and coaches of all levels.
     Diane G. Miller: International & National Coach

I have always gotten very nervous during competitions and tests, but by using the techniques and exercises provided by this book, I am able to skate so much better and have a blast! I recommend it to every athlete.
     Kim Navarro: International Competitor & U.S. Olympic Team Alternate

I really appreciate Choeleen's words to the parents. My husband and I are Katy's biggest fans and supporters, so it is great to have an expert's advice on how to handle this very important role.
     Tammy Taylor: Mother of World Junior Medalist Katy Taylor

More amazing than the original! . . . The information is clearly organized for athletes, coaches, and parents, and provides useful examples from real skaters' lives. Choeleen did an awesome job.
     Tom Zakrajsek: International & National Coach

UPDATED, SECOND EDITION

THE INNER CHAMPION

A Mental Toughness Training
Manual for Figure Skaters

*Choeleen
Loundagin,* M.A.

© 1997, 2004 by Choeleen Loundagin
All rights reserved. No part of this manuscript may be used, reproduced or transmitted in any form or by any means, electronic or mechanical, without written permission from the author except in the case of brief quotations embodied in critical articles and reviews.

Publisher:
InnerChamp Books
P.O. Box 11362
Santa Rosa, CA 95406
www.innerchamp.com

Author:
Choeleen Loundagin
choeleen@innerchamp.com
phone: 707-571-8023
fax: 707-546-3764

Copyeditor: Trish Medalen
Illustrations & Cover Design: MaryKate Adair
Layout and Design: Critical Eye Design

Library of Congress Control Number: 2004096259
ISBN: 0-9663949-6-8
First Edition: August 1997
Second Edition: November 2004, updated

Library of Congress Cataloging-in-Publication Data

Loundagin, Choeleen.
    The inner champion : a mental toughness training manual for figure skaters / Choeleen Loundagin. -- 2nd ed.
        p. cm.
    Includes bibliographical references and index.
    ISBN 0-9663949-6-8
    1. Skating--Psychological aspects.
    2. Skating--Training.
    I. Title.

GV852.3.P75L68 2004   796.91'2
QBI04-200344

To every athlete, coach, and parent dedicated to living life as an Inner Champion.

Some of my favorite inspirational sayings:

You can't catch smoke.
(My dad used this phrase to remind me that
when I do my best, it is as if I am smoking hot,
and like smoke, I can't be caught.)

*Give your best to the world and
the best will come back to you.*

*You miss **100%** of the chances
you don't take.*

*No matter what happens,
the people who count will always love you.*

*You have no chance of success
if you never try.*

*For every door that slams shut, another door
(or sometimes even a window) is open.*

*If at first you don't succeed,
try again another way.*

Sometimes you have to laugh or else you will cry.

*In all the history of the world, there has never
been an Inner Champion exactly like
YOU!*

Contents

Acknowledgments
Preface to the updated, second edition
Introduction: What is an Inner Champion?

1 *Mental toughness basics*. **19**
   Why is mental toughness important? 19
   What are mental skills? 21
   How do mental skills work? 22
   The mind-body connection 23
   How the mind-body connection works 24
   Creating good habits 25
   Mental skills and practice 26
   Mental toughness: final round 27
   Message to coaches and parents 27
   Mental toughness training exercises. **28**

2 *Turn your dreams into reality*. **31**
   The importance of goal setting 32
   Start with a mission statement 34
   SMART and Positive goal setting 36
   Creating goals 40
   The Inner Champion Circle 41
   Work together to set goals 42
   Affirmations and imageries 44
   Goals for events 44
   Evaluate yourself and your goals 45
   Team missions and goals 47
   Goal-setting exercises 48
   Goals: final round 49
   Message to coaches and parents 50
   Mental toughness training exercises **59**

3 Think like an Inner Champion 65
  Confidence and the power of your thoughts 66
  Self-talk control 67
  Change your perception 68
  Use thought stoppage 70
  Change stinking thinking to Inner Champion thoughts .. 71
  Counter persistent stinking thinking 72
  Take a time-out to be negative 73
  Imagine your stinking thinking away 73
  Change irrational and distorted thoughts 76
  Use self-talk control for more than confidence 77
  Increase confidence with additional methods 79
  Is it possible to be too confident? 81
  Self-talk control, confidence, and life 81
  Self-talk control: final round 82
  Message to coaches and parents 83
  Mental toughness training exercises 86

4 To relax or energize? That is the question 91
  Not everyone is the same 92
  Optimal activation level 93
  Fight or flight response 93
  Relaxation 94
  Energizing 103
  Activation: final round 106
  Message to coaches and parents 106
  Mental toughness training exercises 110

5 Use the power of your imagination 115
  Introduction to imagery 116
  How imagery works 117
  Types of imagery 118
  How to practice imagery 119
  Different uses of imagery: the three P's 120
  Imagery for team skaters 122
  Imagery: final round 123
  Message to coaches and parents 124
  Mental toughness training exercises 126

6 Stay focused **131**
  Control your attentional focus 132
  Make focusing easier 134
  Identify distractions 135
  Deal with distractions 136
  Recover from mistakes 139
  Increase your attentional focus endurance 140
  Change your type of focus 141
  Attentional focus for team skaters 142
  Attentional focus: final round 142
  Message to coaches and parents 143
  Mental toughness training exercises **149**

7 Take action to enhance healing **155**
  Goals 156
  Self-talk 157
  Activation control 157
  Imagery 158
  Attentional focus 159
  Seek out others for further support 159
  Enhanced healing for team skaters 160
  How to use mental skills when you resume training ... 160
  Enhanced healing: final round 162
  Message to coaches and parents 163

8 Control pain with mental toughness **165**
  Self-talk 166
  Activation control 166
  Imagery 167
  Attentional focus 168
  Dealing with pain: final round 168
  Message to coaches and parents 169

9 Perform like an Inner Champion **171**
  Preparation for events 171
  Plan of action during events 178
  Plan of action when events are over 183
  Inner Champion performance: final round 185
  Message to coaches and parents 185
  Mental toughness training exercises **191**

CONTENTS

10 *Make a commitment to be an Inner Champion* .. **197**
    Make a full-time commitment 198
    Continue your mental toughness training 199
    Learn life lessons 199
    Overcome challenges the Inner Champion way 200
    Make a commitment: final round 201
    Message to coaches and parents 201
    Mental toughness training exercises **203**

Appendix
    End notes. 207
    Glossary. 213
    Resources and recommendations. 217
    Index. 221
    About the author. 226
    More information. 227

Acknowledgments

They say it takes a village to raise a child; I say it takes a village to raise an author and create a book. Many amazing people have influenced my life and contributed – either directly or indirectly – to the creation of the updated, second edition of *The Inner Champion*. Unfortunately, it would be impossible to acknowledge all of these people, but I would like to specifically express my appreciation for the following individuals:

My entire family is a fantastic source of unconditional love and support. My dad was the first to show me how to use the power of my mind to stop being scared, and instead be excited, about testing and competing. My mom is always reminding me of the importance of having fun while striving to reach my goals. Both my parents taught me that I can do anything I put my mind to. They also taught me that once I decide to pursue something, I should do my best and make it BIG!

My sister Lisa's high ambitions and driven nature are admirable, and she never stops reminding me of the need to treat myself as I would my best friend. My brother Sean thinks more highly of me than anyone and has been like a rock for me throughout my life. His commitment to motivating the children in his community is inspiring. I am in awe watching my niece, Rhiannon, and my nephew, Tyler, pursue their passions and dreams – I marvel at their resilient spirit, playfulness, and determination.

My Auntie is a wonderful combination of sweetness and strength – she is the soft spot in my life when things get hard. Doug, Jeanne, and my uncle Mike are forever supportive, and my cousins Tim and Chris never hesitate to help me in any way they can. My godmother Jeanne is my angel, my cousins Wendy and Sheila are an endless source of fun and adventure, and my godchildren, Nicole, T.C., Jocelyn, Emily, and Michael, help me keep life in perspective – I am blessed to be a part of their lives.

Ulysses van der Kamp has the remarkable ability to help me restore peace and balance in my life when my never-ending projects become overwhelming. His patience, love, and understanding have also had a significant influence on my writing process, and he and his family have provided me with a fabulous writing environment and nonstop encouragement.

Three of my former coaches are also a part of my family. Skippy Baxter was my first coach, and I know my life would be different if he hadn't been there to guide me in my first steps on the ice (and for years later). I am fortunate to see him still nearly every day. My primary coach, Candy Aylor-Morris, taught me the value of striving to reach my potential no matter what I do, and she is an extraordinary friend who continues to support my every endeavor. Faye Ghielmetti has believed in me and encouraged my various pursuits throughout the years, is extremely loyal and an outstanding listener, and can always make me laugh!

Jennifer Hutcheon-Leon has been a close friend longer than anyone, and she is my best salesperson; Lisa Mitchell is my grounding force and sounding board; and Chris Wakefield is one of the most optimistic and energetic people I know. Donna Firenzi helped create the title of my book; Cary Davalos taught me the fine art of networking; and Michelle Van Dyke is the epitome of mental toughness. My colleagues at Snoopy's Home Ice are tireless supporters, as is Tom Mitchell, who shares my passion for bringing out the best in people.

My editor, Trish Medalen, is talented, thorough, and patient. Her strong commitment to quality and her belief in this project have been invaluable. Chris Mitchell has been an essential source of feedback throughout the writing process. Several skaters, coaches, and parents added great value to this book through their peer reviews, ideas, and quotes.

Lastly, I am grateful to the athletes, coaches, and parents who have allowed me to play a role in their quest for excellence. Working with and learning from these dedicated, passionate people is truly inspiring!

Preface to the Updated, Second Edition

Experts know that what sets champion skaters apart is their ability to master the mental game – to maintain confidence and focus despite pressures and distractions. Fortunately, skaters can easily learn the techniques and develop the skills that will let them perform at their very best with the updated, second edition of *The Inner Champion: A Mental Toughness Training Manual for Figure Skaters*.

This manual appeals to skaters of all ages and disciplines who want to realize their potential both on and off the ice. It is also a practical guide for coaches and parents wishing to enhance the total skating experience of their students and children. The second edition retains the unique characteristics that made the first edition so popular in the world of skating – it's written in the language of figure skaters, it's easy to read, the mental toughness training exercises make the manual fun to use, and the information applies to pursuits both on and off the ice. The second edition is enhanced with supporting quotes from top skaters, their parents, and their coaches; additional techniques and exercises; more in-depth explanations; extensive advice for team skaters; and a wide variety of information included particularly for the reference of coaches and parents.

It should be noted that recreational skaters can also benefit from using Inner Champion techniques. Although many references to performing (in competitions, tests, shows, critiques, exhibitions, etc.) are made throughout this manual, the information pertains to all skaters interested in realizing their potential, regardless of whether they participate in the variety of competitive events available.

The quotes included throughout the book offer inspiring insight into what prominent skaters, as well as their coaches and parents, do to bring out the best in themselves and those around them. The additional techniques, expanded mental toughness training exercises, and more involved explanations in the second edition reflect current research as well as my development as an Athletic Performance Enhancement Consultant. The more I work with skaters and other athletes, the more I learn about the best tools for bringing out the champion that is inside every person.

Of course, many skaters today contribute their mental and physical skills to a team effort. Pair and dance skaters continue to be a constant in skating, while participation in synchronized skating and theatre on ice teams is growing rapidly. In recognition of the increased popularity of team skating and the fact that skating with a partner or group adds another challenging dimension to peak performing, advice specific to *team skaters* – those who skate as a team with **one or more people** – has been included throughout the second edition. If such a distinction is not made in the text, the information presented is applicable to both single and team skaters.

The second edition contains a *message* at the end of each chapter, which is directed expressly to the most important members of a skater's support team – coaches and parents. These messages explain how coaches and parents can best assist their students and/or children in their pursuit of mental toughness and athletic excellence. Even though reading the message alone is beneficial, it is recommended that coaches and parents read each chapter in its entirety to get the most out of the information presented. If you are an adult skater whose parents are not fully involved in your skating, apply the parent information to yourself or a significant other, as appropriate.

Although *The Inner Champion* is written in the language of figure skating, it is important for parents to realize that the various guidelines and exercises can be applied to enhance performance in and enjoyment of other pursuits with minimal effort. Coaches and parents will find helpful suggestions regarding how to use mental skills to improve their own lives, as well.

A noteworthy enhancement that I hope readers will find both instructive and entertaining is the vignettes illustrating the impact mental toughness (or the lack of mental toughness) can have on a skater. At the beginning of chapters two through six, you will find stories about four skaters named Nettie, Newt, Polly, and Pete. Nettie and Newt are pessimistic: they don't expect a lot from themselves, they can hardly tolerate frustrations, and they rarely enjoy themselves on the ice. Their overall negative attitudes coupled with a lack of mental toughness make it nearly impossible for them to develop their Inner Champion and reach their potential. All of these things have earned them the nicknames Negative Nettie and Negative Newt.

Polly and Pete are optimistic: they expect the best from themselves, and they enjoy the thrill of facing challenges as well as pushing themselves to healthy limits. Their mental toughness and overall positive attitude make it highly possible for them to reach their potential. All of these things have helped them develop their Inner Champion and earned them the nicknames Positive Polly and Positive Pete. Their stories are told to help readers understand how their thoughts, emotions, reactions, and behaviors all affect how much fun and success they experience while they skate. Readers might recognize themselves in some of the stories, and they may wish they were more like Polly and Pete and less like Nettie and Newt. Fortunately, everyone can control his or her thoughts, emotions, reactions, and behaviors to become mentally tough just like Polly and Pete, and this manual can help readers learn how.

The worksheets from the first edition have been redesigned as mental toughness training exercises that can be completed in the reader's own self-designed mental toughness training journal. The fun, easy-to-follow exercises still provide the opportunity to immediately apply the information contained in the manual. However, in contrast to the one-time usage offered by the original worksheets, maintaining a journal will encourage the ongoing development of mental toughness training throughout a skater's career. Although it is not necessary to read all the chapters in order, it is best to read each chapter in its entirety and complete the exercises for that topic before moving on to a different chapter.

The second edition is well organized with headings and subheadings to make following the information effortless. New additions include the *Preface;* the introduction, *What Is an Inner Champion?;* and the final chapter, *Make a Commitment to Be an Inner Champion*. The manual's introductory text is followed by detailed information regarding the development of a variety of mental skills and techniques. The remainder of the manual contains specific information pertaining to the use of mental skills to enhance performances at events, healing, comebacks, and pain management. Each chapter now concludes with a *Final Round* section that summarizes the information presented in the chapter. The *Index* and *Glossary* add to the ease of using the manual, and the *Resources and Recommendations* is an excellent guide for readers who desire supplemental information.

The additions and updated information, as well as the unique qualities that made the first edition an immediate success, allow the second edition of *The Inner Champion* to maintain the designation of being an exceptional resource that can be used throughout a skater's career to win the mental game.

                                           C.L.
                                           Santa Rosa, CA, 2004

Introduction: What Is an Inner Champion?

Everyone has a champion inside, and your Inner Champion is just waiting to be discovered.

The definition of an Inner Champion has nothing to do with medals, titles, fame, or money, although those things may come with having a well-developed Inner Champion. Inner Champions have an incredible passion for their sport and want to do everything in their power to discover how great they can be. They find learning and improving fun, thrive on challenges, and enjoy pushing themselves to their healthy limits. They trust their coaches' instruction, and they communicate freely with their coaches, parents, teammates, trainers, and any others contributing to their quest to be their best. Inner Champions treat themselves as they would treat a best friend and know that it is as important to be a good sport as it is to be a good athlete. They take pleasure in sharing their love of their sport with an audience and, when the time comes, appreciate the opportunity to be a role model.

Perhaps the most important characteristic of an Inner Champion is being mentally tough. Inner Champions are confident, expect great things of themselves, and have learned how to handle pressure. They maintain an optimistic perspective even when times get rough and view mistakes as learning experiences. In fact, what some see as setbacks, they see as opportunities to grow. They practice with a purpose, make every movement count, and know exactly what they want to accomplish every day. Inner Champions stay in the moment, keep focused on what they can control, and successfully deal with distractions on a daily basis. They are disciplined yet playful, don't rely on others for motivation, and use the power of their imagination, thoughts, and emotions to bring out the best in themselves. Inner Champions are not perfect, but they have learned how to bring out their best even in the most difficult situations. If you want to be able to define yourself as an Inner Champion, this manual is for you.

Everyone – including you – can develop his or her Inner Champion. It is just a question of how important it is to you, and more significantly, how much effort and energy you are willing to put out. Because many positive qualities of an Inner Champion come from being mentally tough, mental toughness training is one aspect of your development that you can't ignore if you want to be able to look back at your skating career and know that you did everything possible to reach your potential.

Even if all you want out of skating is simply to have fun, you can use this manual to enhance your enjoyment on the ice by focusing on the mental skills that interest you most. For those of you aiming for more, however, the contents of this manual can help you become the best skater – as well as the best person – you can be.

Chapter 1

Mental Toughness Basics

> *Athletes often . . . [place] far too little emphasis on the most important factor: their minds. . . . Mental preparation is the key to achievement on every level, in every endeavor, by every individual.*
> **Bernard Ford: World Dance Champion & Olympic Coach**

The Inner Champion: A Mental Toughness Training Manual for Figure Skaters is designed to help you strengthen your mental toughness and discover your Inner Champion. If you make a commitment to read the manual and complete the various exercises, as well as review the information annually and apply what you learn on a daily basis, you will become more mentally tough. Consequently, you will increase the control you have to reach your athletic potential, have more fun while you skate, and be able to enjoy the process and rewards of being an Inner Champion.

Why is mental toughness important?

Mental toughness is much more than just a desirable trait – it is as necessary to your skating success and enjoyment as learning good technique and using smart training habits. It is easy to find examples of highly talented skaters who rarely perform their best because they lack mental toughness and are unable to perform under pressure or deal with distractions. In contrast, the skaters who are mentally tough enough to handle the stress and challenges that their sport presents most often perform up to their potential and are able to truly enjoy skating.

As changes take place in the sport of figure skating, the pressure and distractions skaters can face seemingly multiply every season. The high cost of training, potential rewards for skating well, and increasingly intense levels of competition are the most obvious sources of pressure and distractions.

While the cost and demands of training continue to increase, so do the possible rewards – most of which can offset the potentially tremendous expense of skating. In fact, financial rewards for performing well (and even for showing the promise of future success) have never been greater in this sport and are now available to skaters very early in their careers. Rewards in the form of assignments to National and International events, as well as invitations to elite training camps, are sometimes just as desirable as financial support because they offer greater exposure and experience, which are invaluable for continued success. Unfortunately, rewards in the form of competition earnings, endorsement and show contracts, invitations and assignments, and financial support from skating federations and sponsors can easily overwhelm athletes who lack mental toughness. All too often, when not dealt with properly these rewards become more of a distraction and source of stress than the opportunity they were meant to be.

In addition to training costs and reward opportunities, skaters in every discipline and level, from Pre-Preliminary to Championship events, are continuously challenged by an ever-increasing level of competition. Strong technical ability or outstanding style alone is no longer sufficient to ensure success in competition. In order to be successful as a competitive single skater, an athlete must be equally strong in jumps, spins, edges, stamina, musical interpretation, and acting, and should anticipate the technical bar to rise each year. Successful pairs are expected to have the ever-expanding qualities of single skaters, as well as to be able to do increasingly dangerous lifts and demanding throws.

Besides exhibiting continuously inventive and challenging footwork, edge quality, and choreography, ice dancers are required to perform well-rounded, athletic programs with elements from singles and pairs. Successful synchronized teams must add variety and difficulty to their elements as teams push the limits each year, and theatre on ice teams must reinvent themselves with greater creativity every season. As demanding as all this is, it is essential that skaters from all disciplines meet these difficult expectations with the appropriate expression on their face throughout their entire performance (no grimaces or obvious gasps for air, please!). Other factors that can be experienced as pressure and distractions instead of challenges are the ever-increasing length of the competitive season, constant rule changes, and the fact that many competitions require multiple elimination rounds in a short amount of time.

As skaters are asked to meet the challenges offered by the sport at each level, it is easy to see why mental toughness is essential. It is not enough for competitors to focus primarily on the physical aspects of training, along with a secondary emphasis on musical interpretation. The mental side of the sport must be addressed for athletes to actualize their skating capabilities, and – perhaps more vital to the longevity of their careers – to have fun while doing so. However, before you can become mentally tough and discover your Inner Champion, you must understand what mental toughness is and how mental skills work. The remainder of this chapter will focus on these topics.

What are mental skills?

In order to be mentally tough, you must learn and develop mental skills. Mental skills are something that you probably already use, but you might not know you are using them. Or you might use them without having the level of control you would like. For example, sometimes you might feel more confident than at other times, and concentrating may be easy one day and then difficult the next day. If you've ever practiced a conversation you expected to have, or if you've gone over in your mind how you might ask for something in order to get the answer you want, you have used mental skills.

Mental skills separate an outstanding athlete from a good athlete. If two skaters with the same type of physical training are equally talented, the one who is mentally tougher will be more consistent and experience greater success. In all sports, some athletes do well under pressure and others choke when it really counts. The reason for this is not physical in nature; it has to do with their mental toughness.

There is far more to using mental skills than just thinking positively. Mental skills involve setting useful goals, communicating well with the people contributing to your success, controlling your thoughts, emotions, and perceptions, maintaining a champion-like attitude, knowing when and how to relax and energize yourself, using the power of your imagination, knowing what to focus on, being able to deal with distractions, and managing your time well. All of these skills are explained throughout the manual, and exercises are provided to help you develop each one. Fortunately, mental skills can be learned and used by people of different ages and skill levels.

How do mental skills work?

A skater does not skate her best because she gets lucky or because it just happens that way. Likewise, a good skater doesn't skate poorly because he is very unlucky, has bad karma, or forgets how to skate. Skating your best, which is called having a *peak performance*, *optimal performance*, or *being in the zone*, is the result of your mind and body working together. If you improve your mental skills while you improve your physical skills, you will be able to control how well your mind and body work together.

Following are some questions to think about before you read more about mental skills:

- Have you ever had a peak performance? What was it like? Why do you think it happened?

- Have you ever choked during a test or competition? Have you ever had a horrible day at practice? What was that like? Why do you think it happened?
- Do you believe you can learn how to control how you skate each day?

When you finish reading about mental toughness, be sure to complete the exercises at the end of this chapter regarding your best and worst performances. This will help you discover what does and does not work for you to skate your best.

The mind-body connection

We often think of our minds and bodies as being separate, but there is a connection between the mind and body. Your mind (perceptions, thoughts, emotions, etc.) affects your body (muscle coordination, energy level, etc.) and vice versa. Have you ever heard of someone doing something that under normal circumstances would be near impossible, but they did it because it was extremely important at the time? For example, there was an elderly lady who lifted up a car to save her grandchild when the youngster became pinned under it. Under normal circumstances, that lady wouldn't have been able to push a car, let alone lift one. But she knew she had to save her grandchild, and she was so determined that all her mental and physical energy focused on lifting the car. This is a great example of the mind and body working together.

An example of the mind working against the body is telling yourself not to fall. Chances are that if you go into an element thinking, *Don't fall!,* you probably will fall, because the main message is *FALL!* Likewise, being physically tired often makes you mentally tired, which is an example of your body working against your mind. You cannot be mentally tough without learning how to control the mind-body connection. However, before learning how to control this connection, you must have a better understanding of how the connection between your mind and body works.

How the mind-body connection works

Your **perceptions** result in **thoughts**, your thoughts result in **emotions**, and the combination of all three leads to neurochemical changes in your brain. Your brain chemistry can affect your mental and physical performance in a positive or negative manner, because neurochemicals are what the brain uses to communicate both within the mind and with the body. Brain chemistry can affect a variety of areas including coordination, balance, timing, muscular control, ability to focus, and energy level.

Sometimes the physical reaction to your perceptions, thoughts, and emotions is so minor that you don't even notice, but other times the reaction is intense. For example, when you view a situation as being something that you can easily handle, you may experience calm and confident thoughts and emotions. You may notice your body feels extra strong, you may relax a little, or maybe you won't notice any changes at all. However, when you are in a situation that you view as threatening, you may experience thoughts and emotions of doubt and fear. You might feel your heart race, your muscles may shake, and you may start to sweat more than usual.

Although the mind is critical to your performance, you must not forget that the mind-body connection works both ways. Body conditions, such as hydration, nutrition, pain, rest, and conditioning, are communicated to the brain using a variety of biochemicals. These conditions and resulting communications can positively or negatively affect your perceptions, thoughts, and emotions, and finally, your performance. Poor nutrition, lack of sleep, weak training habits, and dehydration will do little to boost your performance, whereas being properly fueled, well rested, conditioned, and hydrated with plenty of fluids will free your mind and body to focus on getting the job done.

Fortunately, you can learn how to control the connection between your mind and body with the proper mental and physical training. You can choose how you perceive a situation, just as you can learn to control your thoughts, emotions, behaviors, and (for the most part) the condition of your body.

Understanding how the mind-body connection works makes it easy to imagine how a simple change in perception can dramatically enhance or weaken your performance. For example, perceiving a single situation as either something to dread or a challenge you are excited to overcome will have nearly opposite effects on your performance. In fact, how you perceive, think, feel, and react to a situation will have a much greater impact on your performance than the situation itself.

The mental skills covered in this manual will help you develop control of the mind-body connection so you can enjoy yourself while you skate your best more consistently. Once you start mental toughness training, your days of relying on Lady Luck for a great skate will be numbered. Instead, you will be able to depend on the champion within you.

Creating good habits

Take time to develop strong mental skills and create good habits necessary to control your mind-body connection. Doing so is essential to your success because when you are under stress, your mental and physical habits – both positive and negative – will surface. Therefore, choose to perceive each situation you face in the best way possible, and practice controlling your thoughts, emotions, and reactions throughout the day – every day – both on and off the ice. For example, if you have the habit of reacting to difficulties with fear, frustration, or the desire to give up, make an effort to perceive the situation as a challenge you can overcome. In such a situation, purposely react in a calm, confident manner while you focus on a solution instead of the problem. You can actually enjoy challenges and feel energized instead of threatened if you respond with courage rather than fear. Consistency in perception is necessary in order to stay off the emotional roller coaster that can lead to many unnecessary ups and downs in your performance level.

Because the mind-body connection works both ways, your body language and how you act will bring about thoughts and emotions that reflect your behavior. For example, if you feel a bit tired and you choose to give in to the feeling by acting tired, you will think more about how tired you are and soon will feel even worse. However, if you maintain good posture, keep your movements quick, and think about what you are doing instead of how you feel, you will soon feel better. Likewise, if you act in a confident manner by skating tall, holding your head high, and keeping a calm yet determined expression on your face, it will be easier to feel confident, even if you started out with self-doubts. Follow these four principles to create Inner Champion habits:

- Act how you want to feel.
- Talk the talk and walk the walk of an Inner Champion to get what you want out of life.
- Think it, see it, believe it, act it, and do it.
- If you are going to do something, give your best effort!!

Mental skills and practice

It is important to understand that the mental skills covered in this manual can help you control the mind-body connection, but they are not magic! Without the proper technique and physical training, even the most mentally tough athlete will not be able to accomplish very much. In addition, mental skills are like physical skills and require time and practice to learn before you see a difference. You would not expect to pass a skating test without practice or learn a double axel during your first week of private lessons, so don't expect any miracles just from reading this mental toughness training manual. Mental toughness depends on mental skills that need to be learned, practiced, and utilized in order to get the most out of them.

You must also remember that only you can control such important factors as your thoughts, actions, and emotions. Your coach and this manual can teach you the skills you need to know to reach your potential as a skater, but it is up to you to practice the skills and use them. The results of your mental toughness training will reflect how much energy, effort, and time you are willing to give. If you want to see your best, give your best. It will be well worth it!

Mental toughness: final round

All mental skills can be used to help you in different areas of your life. For example, you can use these skills to prepare for a test in school or to give a speech. In the work world, you can use mental skills to prepare for an audition, interview, presentation, or business meeting. You can also improve your concentration in class, meetings, and lectures, or while reading. You can even improve your communication with your family and friends by using mental skills. Examples of these applications are pointed out throughout the manual.

Message to coaches and parents

It is never too soon or too late to introduce the basics of mental skills to children and adults. Skaters who learn these skills at a young age or when they first start skating can often prevent or minimize performance problems associated with the lack of confidence common in teenagers and the intensified pressure encountered at higher levels of competition. If your students or children already use mental skills, encourage them to discover additional methods to increase their ability to learn, improve, and perform their best. Ask them to develop new techniques to deal with situations, pressures, and distractions that will arise as they move up through the ranks. Even the rare athletes who seem to have an innate ability to deal with nerves and outside pressures can learn how to enhance the skills they already use with mental toughness training.

Keep in mind that mental skills take time and practice before the benefits become noticeable. Encourage your skaters to be patient! Make mental toughness training an integral part of development for your students and children, and encourage the use of these skills in all areas of life! Be creative in applying these skills to enhance your own life, as well.

Mental Toughness Training Exercises

Create a mental toughness training journal

The first exercise in this manual, creating your own personalized mental toughness training journal, should be completed before you do any other exercise. It is a good idea to use a three-ringed binder, so you can add paper and change the order of the contents whenever you need to. Pick a binder size that will fit in your skate bag. Try to find a style that has clear pockets on the outside to hold pictures, a page of your favorite sayings, or a collage that you can make. Be creative, and design your journal to reflect the athlete and person you want to be, your Inner Champion. Start with plenty of paper, because the majority of the exercises in the manual ask you to write lists, answer questions, or record your experiences.

Think about your best and worst performances

Think back to your worst performance during a competition. Write your answers to the following questions in your mental toughness training journal. If you have never competed or have only skated your best during a competition, think of a test or practice that did not go well.

1. What were you thinking about? Describe the thoughts you remember having before, during, and after you skated. Did these thoughts seem to help the situation or make it worse?
2. What were you concentrating on before, during, and after you skated?
3. How did your body feel before, during, and after you skated? How did your muscles feel? What was your breathing like? Did you have butterflies in your stomach? Were you hot or cold? Were you shaking? Did you feel in control of your body?
4. Did you feel prepared before the competition? Explain how you were and were not prepared.
5. In the future, what would you do differently? Why?
6. In the future, what would you do the same? Why?

7. Is there anything else you can remember about the experience?

Now think back to your best performance during a competition. Write your answers to the following questions in your mental toughness training journal. If you have never competed or have never skated your best during a competition, think of a test or practice that went extremely well.

1. What were you thinking about? Describe the thoughts you remember having before, during, and after you skated. Did these thoughts seem to help the situation or make it worse?
2. What were you concentrating on before, during, and after you skated?
3. How did your body feel before, during, and after you skated? How did your muscles feel? What was your breathing like? Did you have butterflies in your stomach? Were you hot or cold? Did you feel in control of your body?
4. Did you feel prepared before the competition? Explain how you were and were not prepared.
5. In the future, what would you do differently? Why?
6. In the future, what would you do the same? Why?
7. Is there anything else you can remember about the experience?

Keep the answers to these questions in mind as you go through the various chapters in the manual. This information should help you realize which mental skills need the most practice. Also, remember what has worked for you in the past, and be sure to keep repeating it.

Describe an Inner Champion

Think about what it means to be an Inner Champion. Start a list in your mental toughness training journal to describe the ultimate Inner Champion. Make your description more complete by adding to your list as you think of more items. If you have a hard time getting started, review the introduction to this manual.

Be an Inner Champion

Once you start your list describing an Inner Champion, begin each day by asking yourself what you can do to bring out your Inner Champion. Make an effort to have your thoughts, feelings, and actions fit your description of an Inner Champion every day. Think about yourself as if you are an Inner Champion, imagine you are an Inner Champion, act like an Inner Champion, and ultimately, you will **be** an Inner Champion.

Chapter 2

Turn Your Dreams Into Reality

> Set your goals high, and always keep them in focus. Set smaller goals daily or weekly in order to keep the ball rolling in the right direction. I think if it's something that you really want to pursue, then you've got to put 100% into it and go for it.
> **Kristi Yamaguchi: Olympic, World & U.S. National Champion**

How many skaters do you know who seem to have everything going for them except direction and motivation?

Negative Nettie is one of these skaters. She has excellent coaching available, the financial support and time to train properly, a great deal of talent, and many of the physical attributes skaters desire. However, she hasn't realized her full potential because she has no direction and lacks motivation. Negative Nettie never thinks about why she skates, and she doesn't have any clear expectations for herself. She has a few vague dreams for her skating, but no plans for how to make them come true.

Unfortunately, there are even more factors that keep Negative Nettie from developing her Inner Champion and skating her best. She gets bored quickly during practice, she usually just goes through the motions of skating without applying any purpose, and she spends more time socializing than training with focus. She is often overwhelmed by other skaters and the judges at events, and she rarely enjoys performing in front of people. After poor practices and performances, Negative Nettie doesn't spend any time figuring out what went wrong; instead, she tries to forget the disappointing experience as soon as possible. She doesn't even think about what went right when she skates well; instead she figures she just got lucky. To make matters worse, Negative Nettie's coaches, parents, choreographer, and off-ice trainers all seem to want and work toward different goals.

Positive Pete has decided that his involvement in skating is like being on an important mission. He wrote a paragraph about his skating mission that describes why he skates, the type of person and skater he wants to be, what he wants to get out of skating, and the skating dreams he wants to achieve. He has decided on goals that support his mission, and he has made sure that everyone involved in his skating supports his mission and goals. Going through these steps gives Positive Pete a direction toward which he can aim his efforts and energy, it helps him practice with a purpose each training day, and it provides intense passion for every performance.

Remembering why he skates and exactly what he wants to become helps Positive Pete get through difficult days. His goals to be proud of himself at the end of the day and to learn something from every practice and performance help him use each day to get closer to completing his mission. Positive Pete makes sure he spends time evaluating his practices and performances, because he knows that it is the only way he can discover what works the best for him, what does not bring out his Inner Champion, and what adjustments he should make. Knowing exactly what he wants and why he wants it makes it more likely that Positive Pete will make his skating mission a reality.

The importance of goal setting

Setting goals, working to achieve them, evaluating your efforts, and experiencing success each time you reach your goals are all part of using goal setting as an effective mental skill. The most obvious reason goal setting is essential to your success is that it provides a plan of action for achieving your dreams. Consider for a minute what would happen if you were blindfolded and tried to throw a dart at a target. With the blindfold on you would hit something, but it probably wouldn't be the target you were hoping for. The same is true of skating without specific goals in mind. You can train hard and skate hour after hour, but without clear goals and a plan of action for achieving the goals, you will have little chance of accomplishing what you want.

Goals also make it possible to measure success in terms that you can control, such as your progress, instead of just looking at competition and test results that are not solely under your control. With each goal you achieve, your confidence will be strengthened. This, in turn, can help you feel more aggressive in your skating and improve your consistency. Goals can keep you from getting discouraged or overwhelmed by the many improvements you could make. Sometimes in skating it can seem like your work is never done, because there is always something new to learn or an element to improve. By using goals, you are aware of your progress, as well as what more you can accomplish.

In addition, goals are helpful because they give you a focus, enabling you to perform better and get more out of practice and lessons. If you are focused on what you want to achieve during a performance, it is hard to focus on other things that cause stress and nervousness. While training, Inner Champions can maintain steady improvements by making an effort to practice with a purpose on a daily basis. However, before you can practice with a purpose, your purpose must be clear to you, and goals provide that clarity. Daily practice goals make training time more productive and fun by keeping you motivated and continuously challenged. With no purpose, your practice time can be just a boring exercise of going through the motions. This type of training does nothing to enhance the quality of your skating, because it promotes the development of poor muscle memory and bad habits. It would be better to skate one session with an intense focus and full effort than to skate several sessions during which you simply do repetitions with no goal in mind.

> *I firmly believe in goal-oriented practices. Some skaters . . . focus more on the time they've spent on the ice than on what they've done with that time. Brian always practices with a purpose in mind.*
> **Linda Leaver: Olympic, World & National Coach & longtime coach of Brian Boitano**

There are even more ways in which goal setting can be useful! Setting a variety of practice goals can prevent injuries and frustration by making you less likely to over-train one or two elements. If you are part of a team (dance, pair, synchronized, theatre on ice, etc.), setting goals together can strengthen team cohesion while focusing all efforts in the same direction. Lastly, every time you achieve a goal, you will increase the pride you have in yourself and the satisfaction you experience when you skate. These feelings will fuel your desire to achieve even more!

Start with a mission statement

The first step in making your dreams a reality is creating your own mission statement. A mission statement explains why a person, team, or organization does what he, she, or they do. Your mission statement should explain why you skate and what you want to accomplish. It should also describe what you want to get out of the experience in addition to your accomplishments, as well as what type of skater and person you want to be. Your mission statement can be a few sentences or several paragraphs long. Make sure your mission statement clarifies why you are willing to put out the amount of effort, make all the sacrifices, spend numerous hours training, change your sleep patterns, and do everything else you do to skate.

Creating a mission statement will help you direct your energy and efforts in a passionate, dedicated, disciplined manner. Having a clear mission statement to which you are fully committed will be extremely motivating and enable you to realize your full potential. Once you set out on your mission, you will find that knowing exactly what you want and why you want it leads to far more success than having just vague dreams for unclear reasons.

Because your attitude is a choice, being committed to your mission helps you choose an Inner Champion attitude day after day. It will help you stay focused on all the positive aspects of skating and give you a sense of purpose each day. Being on a mission will keep skating in perspective, especially when times are tough and you feel stressed, frustrated, discouraged, or overwhelmed.

Your mission will create excitement about why you skate and give you the discipline to do what it takes to accomplish your goals, even if you feel tired and low on energy. Just thinking about your mission will remind you of what you get from the sport and why you enjoy it so much. When you keep your mission in mind, you'll find that you enjoy the process of training and performing a lot more. It is hard to feel nervousness, fear, frustration, and other negative emotions when you are focused on your mission.

You can enhance your motivation, intensify your focus, stay in touch with your passion, and maintain your Inner Champion attitude more easily if you post your mission statement in a place where you can read it often. Reading your statement can pump you up before a competition or in the morning before practice. Be certain to read your mission statement before every event throughout the year to ensure that you start with an Inner Champion mindset.

It is easy to see why creating a mission statement and living by it will bring out your Inner Champion. Follow the first mental toughness training exercise at the end of this chapter to create your mission statement. Take the time to update your mission statement yearly, because as you progress as a skater and grow as a person, your mission statement may change.

SMART and Positive goal setting

Once you have a clear mission statement to which you can fully commit, put your statement into action by creating goals. Setting goals guides your decisions regarding what you should do each day to make your mission statement a reality. When setting goals, you should follow six guidelines that are easy to remember if you think of the **SMART** and **P**ositive goal-setting acronym:

> **S**PECIFIC
> **M**EASURABLE
> **A**CTION-ORIENTED
> **R**EALISTIC
> **T**IME BOUND
> & **P**OSITIVE, TOO !

Specific. Specific goals are more motivating and direct your focus better than general objectives. However, thinking about your dreams and other general objectives is a good place to start when setting goals. For example, if you want to skate well during a competition, that can be considered a general objective. Think about what you need to do to accomplish this in specific terms. Focus on the physical aspects of your performance, such as technical elements, your presentation, power, flow, timing, and positions. Also include mental aspects related to your performance, such as your focus, energy level, thoughts, and enjoyment. Set goals that are as specific as possible and follow the other guidelines.

Measurable. Your goals should be measurable so you know for certain when they have been achieved. Having the goal to be your best is hard to measure, because it is difficult to know when you have accomplished that goal. The same is true of the goal to be consistent. You need to ask yourself, *What do I want to do, exactly?* Measurable goals direct your focus in a precise way so that your expectations become quantifiable.

For example, instead of wanting to be more consistent, define your goal as wanting to land nine out of every ten jumps you attempt. To improve your power, focus on the time it takes you to stroke around the rink five times or how much ice you cover during your program. To improve your stamina, focus on how many laps, patterns, or programs you can do in a row before tiring. To improve your presentation, make it a goal to look out to the crowd a certain number of times during each section of your program.

Action-oriented. The ability to achieve your goals should be under your complete control and depend only on your action. Your effort, technique, expression, stamina, enjoyment, and focus are all under your control. For example, the goal to skate a clean short program while focusing on one element at a time is completely under your control. A goal to skate the same program with finesse and strength from start to finish is also under your control.

Avoid outcome goals (the outcome of a test, competition, and so forth), because these are often subject to things out of your control. For example, taking first place in a competition seems like a great goal, but it is not really under your control. The two most obvious elements over which you have no control are how your competitors skate and the opinions of the judges (judging is not always objective and opinions can differ).

> *I think we put a lot of pressure on ourselves . . . to get certain places, and it didn't work out. . . . We learned that we need to skate for ourselves. . . . That is always when things work out best.*
>
> **Todd Sand: Olympian, World Pair Medalist & U.S. National Pair Champion with Jenni Meno**

Imagine a scenario in which you skate your very best, but someone else skates even better, or the judges don't appreciate your program as much as you hoped. You could learn from such an experience by training harder for the next competition in order to compete better with the more advanced skater. You also could find out what the judges didn't like about your skating and try to improve in that area. However, you should feel proud of the fact that you did as well as possible at the time. One drawback of outcome goals is that in a situation such as this, you would feel like you failed if your only goal had been to win. Another problem with outcome goals is that you won't be focused on your own skating if you are thinking about judges' marks or beating other skaters.

If you feel a burning desire to have outcome goals, make sure you back them up with performance goals that will improve the possibility of achieving your outcome goals. For example, back up a goal to win with goals to skate cleanly, have speed, present to the judges well, trust your training, and focus on one element at a time.

Realistic. If you set goals that are too easy, you will probably get bored. On the other hand, if you set goals that are too difficult, you might become discouraged and want to give up. To establish realistic, yet challenging goals, look at what you are capable of now, and set goals that are slightly beyond that. Then do the same thing over and over. For example, if you land one or two combinations out of ten right now, a goal to always land two out of ten is a bit too easy, and a goal to land ten out of ten is too hard. Having a goal to land four out of ten each day for this week, and five or six out of ten each day the next week, and on and on, is more appropriate.

Occasionally, you may need to adjust your goals, and you should be open to this possibility. Sometimes an injury won't permit you to train, or you might get sick right before a competition. This type of situation can alter your ability to achieve the goals you set for yourself. Or sometimes a goal that seemed like a realistic challenge is much harder to achieve than you expected. When this type of situation happens, it is important for you to be able to let go of your original goal and make adjustments to make it realistic again. The key is to be realistic without being too hard or too easy on yourself.

Time bound. You should always set a date or time for each of your goals to be achieved. If you have goals, but you are working only to achieve them *someday*, you won't be very motivated to complete them. Use many short-term goals together with mid-range and long-term goals, similar to a staircase that builds upon itself.

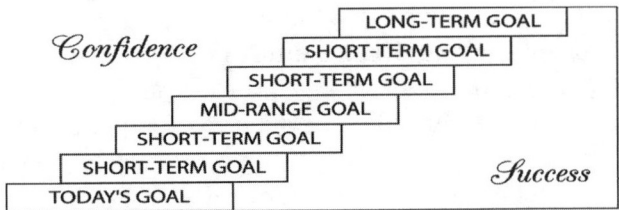

A long-term goal is the end result that you desire, short-term goals are the small improvements you need to make along the way, and mid-range goals connect short-term and long-term goals. Short-term and mid-range goals can help keep you focused and motivated while you're striving for your long-term goal. They will also allow you to experience success often and continuously enhance your self-confidence. It's a great idea to have daily, weekly, monthly, yearly, and career goals.

> *The fact that I can learn new things all the time [keeps me motivated]. . . . I think to keep things fresh and interesting you need to set goals, both short term and long term, and try to achieve them along the way.*
> **Todd Eldredge: Olympian, World & U.S. National Champion**

Positive. Goals should focus on what you want to achieve instead of what you want to avoid. For example, a goal not to fall or not to make a mistake is negative and makes you think about what you don't want to do. In contrast, having a goal to do a clean program makes you think of what you want to do and creates a positive focus.

When you have a goal to change a bad habit, be sure that your goal describes what you want to do correctly. For example, if you want to correct a two-footed landing, make a goal to land on the correct foot by a certain date; if you want to stop rushing your timing on a dance or field move, make a goal to stay on time to the music or to keep an even rhythm during your move;

and if you want to stop bickering with your teammate(s), make a goal to say only supportive comments to your teammate(s).

Creating goals

Now that you understand the importance of having a mission statement with supporting goals and the SMART and Positive guidelines to follow when deciding on your supporting goals, it is time to create your goals! If you have trouble coming up with ideas for goals, try a Star Map. This mental toughness training exercise is explained at the end of this chapter. It is helpful to complete a new Star Map at the beginning of each competitive season. If you participate in more than one discipline, decide on a separate set of goals for each discipline. If you are part of a team, set team goals together and make certain your individual goals are complementary to the team goals. Below are questions you should ask yourself *and steps you should follow* when setting goals:

- What skill do I want to improve to make my mission statement a reality?
- What do I want to do better before I leave the ice today? What is the purpose of my practice?
- What can I do today to make myself more prepared for the next event?
- *Write the goal in your mental toughness training journal.*
- Is the goal specific? Measurable? Under my control? Challenging and realistic? When do I want to achieve it? Does it describe what I want to accomplish? (SMART and Positive?)
- *Rewrite the goal if it does not follow the SMART and Positive guidelines.*
- *Keep track of each goal in your mental toughness training journal on a daily or weekly basis.*
- *Take time to notice your successes and progress. Give yourself rewards for each success you have. A reward can be something simple like telling yourself how well you are doing or spending time with a friend.*

A general but useful goal is to learn something from every practice and performance. You can learn a lot if you evaluate your physical and mental efforts each day. Look for what worked to help you reach your goals and what didn't. Be sure to repeat what worked and change what didn't.

Another powerful goal is to make yourself proud every day. If you decide this goal is practical for you, rate your effort to make yourself proud on a scale from one to ten at the end of each day. Think about the rating you desire as well as your minimum effort requirement. Repeat what gives you the best ratings, and learn from what does not, to bring out your Inner Champion.

The Inner Champion Circle

You can get invaluable input about your goals from your *Inner Champion Circle* – the people who support you and your skating. Every skater should have in the Inner Champion Circle a team of people behind him or her who work well together to offer guidance and support. Your Inner Champion Circle can include many people, such as coaches, parents or guardians, on- and off-ice trainers, a sport psychologist, club and skating federation officials, sponsors, agents, siblings, friends, significant others, school officials, employers, arena management, and anyone else who contributes financially, emotionally, intellectually, or physically (either directly or indirectly) to your success.

INNER CHAMPION CIRCLE

Everyone in your Inner Champion Circle has a role to fulfill that should be specified by you, your parents, or your lead coach when that person joins the circle. (If you are an adult, you or someone significant in your life might fulfill the role typically assumed by parents.) An exercise at the end of this chapter will help you clarify the roles and responsibilities of each person in your Inner Champion Circle.

> *I have a very strong support system. People I surround myself with are behind me 100 percent. Without that, I don't think anything is really possible.*
> **Johnny Weir: World Junior Champion & U.S. National Champion**

You and everyone in your Inner Champion Circle should view you, your lead coach, and your parents or guardian as the *core*, or leaders, of your circle. As *core members*, your lead coach and parents will be the most involved in your skating and should have the most influence when you need guidance in setting goals or making other decisions about your skating. Therefore, the other members of your circle should be willing to take direction from your lead coach and your parents and be supportive of them just as much as they are of you. If you are part of a team, the team's core will include all the team members, the team members' parents or guardians, and the lead coach(es).

Work together to set goals

Athletes who choose their own goals tend to stay motivated much longer and more intensely than those who have these decisions made for them. Therefore, it is extremely important that you *own* your goals. Owning your goals requires you to make the final decision when setting goals instead of letting someone else decide for you. However, getting input about your goals from your Inner Champion Circle, especially from the core members, is a crucial step in the goal setting process.

Parents and/or other people who support your skating financially and in other ways, such as driving you to appointments, can provide input regarding their ability and willingness to support your goals. When you first start skating and performing, you will need to rely a great deal on your lead coach to direct your goal setting. For example, your coach can explain what is expected of skaters at your level for competitions and tests, as well as how to break down elements into realistic steps. Your coach and, depending on the goal, other professionals in your Inner Champion Circle can tell you if your goals are challenging, realistic, and have an appropriate time frame. These people will also have good ideas about how to put your goals in measurable terms.

Although the more experienced you are, the less input you will need, it will continue to be important to exchange ideas about your goals with your lead coach throughout your skating career. This will not only allow the two of you to work together as a team, but hearing your coach's opinions will also help you get a well-rounded perspective before making final decisions regarding the direction of your skating.

> There are many great coaches, but the person that communicates well with you and has your best interests at heart is the right coach for you. It is amazing what can be accomplished by two people who work together.
> **Audrey Weisiger: Olympic, World & National Coach**

It will be extremely helpful if the core members of your Inner Champion Circle meet every year at the beginning of the season to discuss your mission statement and goals for the new season. This meeting doesn't need to be overly formal and should not feel intimidating. For example, all of you could have a casual meeting in a private area of the rink or at a restaurant. During the meeting, everyone should take part in evaluating how the previous season worked and discuss the plan of action and specific goals for the next season. Be sure to explain changes to your mission, if any, and remember the importance of making the final decision about your own goals.

At the end of the meeting, decide who will make sure that everyone in your Inner Champion Circle understands and can support your mission and goals. Taking these steps will help each person in your circle comprehend what he or she is working for and will direct everyone's efforts in the same direction. If someone in your Inner Champion Circle isn't fully supporting your mission, goals, or core members, you and/or the other core members should discuss the problem with that person immediately!

Affirmations and imageries

After you decide on your goals and write them in your mental toughness training journal, write an affirmation – a positive statement about yourself – for each goal. There is a mental toughness training exercise at the end of the chapter to help you do this. Write each affirmation as though you already achieved the goal. For example, if your goal is to skate a clean long program eight out of ten times, write the affirmation, *I skate my long program cleanly*, or, *I have consistent jumps (spins, footwork, etc.) in my program.*

After writing your affirmations in your mental toughness training journal, write them on sticky notes and post them in places that you will see often. For example, post them in your bedroom, in your bathroom, or in your car. Every time you see the notes, be sure to read the affirmations, think about them, and imagine yourself doing what the affirmations state.

Besides imagining the affirmations when you see the sticky notes, it is helpful to imagine yourself being successful when you write your goals in your mental toughness training journal. You should also imagine yourself achieving your goals on the way to the rink (unless you are the one driving), while you are getting ready to skate, when you check on your progress in your mental toughness training journal, or anytime you have a free moment. The more you imagine your goals, the more you will believe they are possible, the more motivated you will become, and the sooner you will achieve your goals.

Goals for events

At least one month before an event, decide what you want to accomplish during your performance. Be sure to focus on a variety of things, such as technique, presentation, mental skills, and having fun. Write these goals in your mental toughness training journal and post affirmations for your goals in your house. If you are traveling to the event, post your mission statement and affirmations all around where you are staying. Remind yourself of your mission statement, goals, and affirmations before and during the event when you need a confidence boost or a more intense focus.

Evaluate yourself and your goals

Evaluate your practices and performances in terms of your goals often and record your evaluations in your mental toughness training journal. This is the best way to stay aware of your progress and learn from your experiences. Celebrate your successes, and figure out what changes need to be made if you did not reach your goals as expected. When you don't reach a goal, allow yourself to be disappointed, sad, or angry, but only for a short amount of time. Beating yourself up and wallowing in sadness, anger, frustration, and disappointment indefinitely will do you no good. Be sad, then learn the lesson, and be glad to move on. **Forget the mistake, but remember the lesson!**

After every event, review your goals to help you evaluate whether you accomplished what you intended. If you were successful, congratulate yourself on a job well done and celebrate! If you missed some goals, look for reasons why you didn't do as well as expected (maybe your goals weren't realistic, you didn't train hard enough, you got distracted, etc.). Try to learn from disappointing experiences by determining what you had control of that you can change in the future. Then make those changes so you can do better the next time! Keep in mind that judges' marks should not take away from your pride or satisfaction. If you perform well but place low, why allow a group of judges – who are just people, after all – to decide whether you should feel proud of yourself or if the performance was enjoyable?

Inner Champions take credit for the role they play in their disappointments and successes. When evaluating yourself and your goals, making excuses instead of taking responsibility for your disappointments makes it impossible for you to learn from your experiences. When you make excuses and blame others for your disappointments without owning up to your role in the situation, you set yourself up for the same disappointing experience in the future.

For example, if you allow yourself to make the excuse that you can't skate well when you draw first or last in a competition, when Suzie Skater is on the ice, when a certain person is watching, or when you're at a particular rink, you probably won't do any better when faced with a similar situation. Instead of making an excuse, figure out how to handle similar situations that may arise in the future by using information from this manual, your coach, and other experiences. It is equally important to take credit for your successes. If you assume that you just got lucky when you skate well, your confidence will not benefit from your success. Take credit for getting your mind and body to work together, for being well prepared and training hard, and for giving your best effort.

> *I actually liked the feeling that if I made a mistake, I couldn't blame anybody but myself. A lot of skaters get in the habit of blaming their coaches for mistakes that they make. . . . But, to me, the whole point of skating – the freedom of it – depends on being self-reliant.*
>
> **Brian Boitano: Olympic, World & U.S. National Champion**

Keep in mind that evaluating yourself, taking responsibility, and making adjustments is different than criticizing, placing blame, and giving up. A failed goal attempt does not make you a failure, a disappointing performance does not make you a disappointment, and an awful practice does not make you an awful person. Not reaching a goal is a failure only if you don't learn from the experience. If a practice or event does not go as you planned, learn from the experience and move on without judging yourself harshly. It is also a good idea to evaluate your Inner Champion Circle to decide who and what is helping or hurting you in achieving your mission and supporting goals.

Just make certain you don't place blame on members of your Inner Champion Circle as a way to avoid taking personal responsibility for your skating. If you decide a change needs to be made, make a commitment to do so, and make sure you discuss the changes you desire with the core members of your circle.

If you consistently come up short of your goals despite making adjustments, ask yourself if – somewhere deep inside – you are purposely giving less effort than you are able to give. Sometimes people are afraid that they may never be as good as they want to be, so they purposely hold back to have an excuse for not attaining their goals. By doing this, they miss many rewarding experiences, they never realize their full potential, and how great they could be remains forever a mystery. If you think you may be doing this, compare what you are missing to what you are protecting yourself from, and you should realize that you have so much more to gain by giving your all. Go for it, and discover just how strong and wonderful your Inner Champion can be.

Team missions and goals

There are many abundantly talented teams in the world that fail to experience the success of which they are capable simply because the team members all have different goals. This makes it impossible for them to work together effectively. Teams are most successful when all of the members are fully committed to a team mission and work together toward the same goals. Teams should create a Team Mission Statement together and make a Star Map each season to guide team goal creation. This experience will help direct the focus and energy of the team while building team cohesion. If you are part of a team, you should set your own individual goals in addition to setting goals as a team. Be sure that your individual goals are consistent with, and do not undermine, the team goals.

Mutual respect and trust among team members is a must for working well together. Team members don't need to be the best of friends, but everyone should respect each other's efforts and be able to trust one another on the ice. It is also important for everyone on the team to understand his or her role and responsibilities, as well as those of each team member. Knowing what is expected, as well as what is unacceptable, is important for everyone when setting up boundaries and guidelines for team behavior.

> *Tanith and I have the same goals. We're both willing to work as hard as we have to and do the things we need to do to be successful. We both realize that staying together, getting along, and working hard is the only way that's going to happen.*
> **Benjamin Agosto: World Junior Dance Champion & U.S. National Dance Champion with Tanith Belbin**

Naturally, teams will have more people in their Inner Champion Circles than single skaters. With the numerous people, interests, and egos, constant open communication and mutual respect is necessary to create a successful team. Even with excellent communication and great respect, there are bound to be times when not everyone readily agrees about the direction the team should take or how to get there. When disagreements arise, it is invaluable to the success and harmony of the team for everyone – especially the core members of the team's Inner Champion Circle – to keep an open mind to solutions, resolutions, and compromises. Of course, it is essential that everyone keep the best interest of the skaters in mind when reaching compromises.

Goal-setting exercises

To get the maximum positive effect out of the mental skills described in this chapter, complete the various goal-setting exercises on a regular basis. Following is a time frame to use for each of the exercises:

- The mission statement and Star Map exercises should be done at least once annually, at the beginning of each year or season.

- The SMART and Positive goal exercise should be used for all your long-term goals throughout the year.
- The daily goal exercise should be used to keep track of your everyday accomplishments that will eventually lead to attaining your long-term goals. If you don't use this exercise regularly, at least decide on goals in your mind before you skate so that you always practice with a purpose. Doing so will still help you work your way toward achieving your long-term goals.
- The program evaluation chart should be filled out every day you skate your program in order to keep track of your progress and help you set daily goals. You should chart your moves and dances, as well.
- The goals for events exercise should be started about a month before each event you enter, and it should be completed at the end of each event.

Goals: final round

Your mission statement and SMART and Positive goals will help you enjoy the process of becoming the best skater you can be. Commit to your mission and practice with a purpose every day to bring out your Inner Champion. Prepare your mind for practice and events by imagining achieving your goals. Evaluate your efforts in achieving your goals to develop a better understanding of what does and does not work for you. Celebrate your successes, and learn from your mistakes before moving on.

> *My philosophy of skating is that you should enjoy yourself and be willing to persevere. Living that philosophy is how I was able to skate 5,532 consecutive show performances!*
> **Skippy Baxter: National Competitor & Member of the U.S. Figure Skating Hall of Fame**

If you feel a lack of motivation or even dread skating, take a moment to reflect on why you started skating and all the things you first loved about it. Next, remind yourself of your mission and goals and appreciate the opportunity that training and events provide. If you still lack enthusiasm, talk with the core members of your Inner Champion Circle and consider making changes to your schedule and/or your circle of supporters to bring back your passion for skating. As a last resort, consider moving on to a different pursuit. Life is something precious to be respected and enjoyed. To be an Inner Champion, you must live your life with passion.

As is the case with all mental skills, you can use mission statements and goals in your life outside skating. Anytime you have a dream that you want to turn into a reality, create a mission statement and use goal setting to help direct your energy and effort in a practical and productive manner. Decide what you want to accomplish, all the reasons why, what you expect from the process, and what type of person you want to be throughout and at the end of the experience. Then follow the same SMART and Positive goal-setting guidelines as you would in your skating to create goals that support your mission. Fully commit yourself to achieving any mission and supporting goals you create, and you will be amazed at all that you can accomplish. Always keep in mind that to get somewhere, you have to know where you are headed first!

Message to coaches and parents

Coaches:

It takes a team effort to make a skater successful. This team – or *Inner Champion Circle* – will have at its core the skater, the lead coach, and the parents, guardian, or significant other of the skater. Each *core member* has a role to fulfill that is crucial to the effectiveness of the Inner Champion Circle and, ultimately, to the success of the skater. In general terms, the skater is the performer and the focus of the circle, the parents are the skater's biggest fan as well as principal emotional and financial support (of course, the parents are also responsible to raise the child), and the lead coach is the technical expert and skating career guide. A skater's Inner Champion Circle should also include anyone contributing to the success of the skater. The role of these additional members is to support not only the skater, but also the entire core of the Inner Champion Circle.

Communicate clearly with new students and their parents — or guardians or significant others, if appropriate — about what you expect your role and responsibilities to entail, as well as how you see the roles and responsibilities of all members of the Inner Champion Circle. Explain your coaching philosophy, the benefits of participating in the sport of skating, how you define success in terms of the process versus the outcome, and why you coach. Be sure to express your desire for mutual respect, and your commitment to respect the parental role of raising a complete child and not just a skater. It is in your best interest, as well as the skater's, to welcome open communication with the skater and parents while also establishing your boundaries regarding when, where, and how you would like the communication to take place. Include in your discussion any other parameters of the relationship that you feel are important.

> *Let skaters and parents know what you expect from them when you first start a student. Then stick to your standards, because as soon as you let things slide, you're asking for trouble in the three-way relationship.*
> **Barbara Roles-Williams: Olympic Medalist & Olympic, World & National Coach**

At the beginning of each season, have a meeting with each student and his or her parents to discuss the student's mission statement and how each person expects to support the mission. Once a mission statement has been embraced by all of you, work together to set SMART and Positive goals for the season. It is essential for each person to understand what it will take to achieve the goals and to commit to doing his or her part. At the conclusion of the meeting, decide who will communicate the skater's mission statement and goals to all members of the skater's Inner Champion Circle.

To ensure that everyone's efforts are directed toward the same purpose, it is important for the skater's entire Inner Champion Circle to have a clear idea of the skater's mission and goals. To foster a healthy, successful experience, if you or someone in the circle cannot support the skater's mission or goals, compromise or change must be made until everyone in the circle is in agreement. If you coach a team, facilitate a mission statement and goal-creation session with the team at the beginning of each season. Individuals should have their own mission and goals, which should complement the team mission and goals.

Make certain your students know that as a member of their Inner Champion Circle, you will be working together with them to reach *their* skating goals. Less experienced skaters will require more guidance from you when setting goals, but always allow the skater to make the final decision. Choosing their own goals will enhance your students' desire to push themselves to achieve significantly more than will striving to accomplish goals chosen by someone else. Listen to what your students have to say before you give suggestions and feedback, and be honest without placing constrictive limits on what is realistic (this can be a delicate balancing act at times!). Be very clear when communicating what you think the skater must do in order to achieve his or her chosen goals. Throughout the years, your role in this process should change from leader to co-collaborator.

> *I find the longer I am coaching the more I realize that from your students you will be taught. You can't always direct them and take control, sometimes they need to work through things on their own. It's all a part of maturing.*
> **Frank Carroll: Olympic, World & National Coach**

Ask your students to set goals on a daily basis, even if they don't write their daily goals in their journals. Check in with your students at the beginning of a lesson to ensure that there is harmony between your lesson plan and their daily goals. In order to emphasize the importance of evaluating their efforts, take the time once or twice a week to ask your students to rate how well they did in achieving their daily goals. Encourage your students to keep track of their progress in their mental toughness training journals. Rate yourself, too, by evaluating how well you contributed to the success of each day. Determine what you did to help or hinder your students' or teams' missions and goals, as well as your own.

Define success with criteria that skaters can control – such as effort, technique, improvement, and attitude – instead of outcomes that they can't control – such as placement and test results. Do not allow your students to define their personal worth by the success they experience on the ice (avoid doing this yourself, as well). Emphasize that an awful skating performance doesn't make the person awful, and failing to achieve a goal doesn't make a person a failure. When a student doesn't reach a goal, avoid taking personal offense to the disappointment, and help your student learn from the experience before moving on. Review goals with your students before and after every event, and at the end of the season. Use this evaluation process to help your students learn from their experiences as well as to promote their personal development.

> *I always worked hard to make sure Sarah [Hughes] knew we were working together, with the priority being getting better, not getting medals.*
> **Robin Wagner: Olympic, World & National Coach**

Do your best to prevent burnout and loss of passion among your students to counteract the trend that shows many children leaving competitive sports in early adolescence. If you notice a lack of passion or motivation within your students, ask them about it immediately. Common reasons include lack of fun, a disconnect with their mission or coach, pressure from themselves or others to succeed, and too much criticism from a coach, parent, or teammate. Other factors are being bored with easy goals, being overwhelmed with goals that are too difficult, overtraining, multiple injuries, insufficient rest, a lack of focus, and no longer finding joy in skating. Help these students make changes to reconnect with the passion they originally felt for skating.

Lastly, go on your own mission by writing a mission statement that you feel passion for, and create supporting goals related to your performance as a coach. If you don't have passion for what you do, consider making changes.

Parents:

If you and your child haven't done so already, meet with your child's lead coach to discuss the roles, responsibilities, and expectations of your child, the coach, and yourself. Also discuss the expectations for everyone in your child's Inner Champion Circle – all those supporting and contributing to the success of your child.

Respect the coaching role by allowing the coach to do the job you have hired him or her to do. Even if you have technical knowledge of skating, giving your child instruction can be confusing, frustrating, and destructive to your child's motivation to skate. Taking on the coaching role can also diminish your effectiveness in being your child's greatest supporter and biggest fan, as well as weaken the teamwork of the Inner Champion Circle. Likewise, any coach you work with should respect your role as parent and the choices you must make for your child, who not only skates, but who is also a family member, a student, and a developing person with interests outside skating.

Establishing open communication with the lead coach, your child, and others in the circle is essential for effective teamwork and a healthy, successful experience. You and the lead coach should agree upon how, when, how often, and where communication will take place between the two of you. Find a balance between your desire to get the best for your child and respecting the private time, teaching time, and client load of the coach. If you cannot agree on boundaries and expectations, it is unlikely that the relationship will last very long.

Share information that can aid the coach in working with your child. For example, if your child is going through a difficult time in school, a family member is seriously ill, your child has been complaining about pain, or your child is more nervous than normal before an event, let the coach know about it. If you have a problem with the coach, discuss the problem with the coach directly, so it can be resolved as quickly as possible. Avoid drawing your child into any conflicts you have with the coach or discussing conflicts with the coach in front of your child. Doing so can be stressful and confusing for your child because of loyalties to both you and the coach.

Similarly, avoid being drawn into conflicts between your child and your child's coach(es) by encouraging your child to communicate with the coach(es) directly; or be certain to understand both sides before taking on the mediator role. Of course, if you think your child is being mistreated, you should act first by removing your child from the situation before you gather the facts to decide the best way to resolve the matter.

> *Don't put up with mental games from a coach, but allow the coach to do the work he or she was hired to do. There should be no intimidation or dishonesty in the coach's dealings with your child, but it is a coach's role to set high standards and expect improvement.*
> **Carole Yamaguchi: Mother of Olympic, World & U.S. National Champion Kristi Yamaguchi**

Stay aware of why your child wants to skate and why you are willing to support your child's involvement in the sport. Keep in mind that most children initially want to participate in sports for fun and enjoyment, for the challenge of learning new things and mastering skills, to meet people and make friends, for the excitement, to win, for the exercise and fitness, for the recognition, and for the travel. Notice that winning is low on the list and fun is most important!

Your reasons for supporting your child's involvement in skating should include many positive, growth-orientated objectives. Maintaining a level of fitness, experiencing the joy of exercise, increasing body awareness, gaining an appreciation of the body's capabilities, and mastering skills are some of the physical and health benefits skating can provide. Social benefits can include exposing you and your child to a variety of people, involving the entire family in a number of ways, engaging your child in a social activity with contemporaries and those in a position of authority, and enjoying a fun social atmosphere.

Psychological benefits are wide ranging, and can include the ability to deal with success and failure, adaptability, communication skills, competitiveness, confidence, cooperation, courage, creativity, dedication to an activity and goals, desire, discipline, establishing priorities, leadership, mental toughness, moral development, organizational skills, patience, persistence, problem-solving, risk-taking, self-esteem, self-reliance, sportsmanship, stress management, and time management; as well as respect for rules, authority, and contemporaries, and so much more.

Participation in any sport provides a mini-life situation in which children can develop characteristics and skills while learning important lessons that can be applied throughout a successful, fulfilling life. It is easy to lose your healthy perspective of sport participation given the amount of time, money, and effort skating requires. Therefore, these possible benefits are important to keep in mind throughout your child's experience in skating, especially during difficult times when you might find yourself questioning why you ever bought that first pair of skates.

At least once a year, ask your child about his or her mission statement, and discuss what you are willing to do to support the mission. Insist on having a meeting with the lead coach and your child at the beginning of the season or year to discuss your child's mission and goals. Encourage your child to choose his or her own goals for practice and events. The goals should be in agreement with the coach as the technical expert and with you as your child's primary emotional and financial support. If your child is open to it, discuss daily goals before each practice to help prepare his or her mind and body for the day. Some children experience such conversations as pressure, so make sure this type of conversation is welcomed by your child or don't have it.

All goals should be under your child's control to achieve, such as being related to performance and effort, and should be stated in positive terms. For example, making someone else proud or winning is not under a person's control, but making yourself proud or striving to win by giving maximum effort is.

Bribery, fear, intimidation, and punishment are not recommended as methods of motivation because they will inhibit intrinsic motivation (motivation that comes from within and is the most long-lasting form of motivation). If you do use bribery, use it sparingly.

Celebrate performances and effort more than results. Avoid defining the worth of your child by the level of success experienced on the ice, and be certain your child doesn't do this either. Discuss with your child that an awful skating performance doesn't make a person awful, and failing to achieve a goal doesn't make a person a failure. Encourage your child to learn from disappointing experiences and move on as soon as possible. It is equally important that you avoid defining your own worth by your child's success. When evaluating your child, keep in mind that skating is an inherently difficult sport. If you find yourself feeling extremely judgmental and disappointed, put on a pair of skates, and perform in front of an audience and judges to experience (again or for the first time) just how hard it can be!

> *[My Olympic experience] made me believe that with hard work and preparation you can attain your goal. It also made me realize how fortunate I am [that] my folks were there in the good times and the bad times, always supportive and optimistic.*
> **Peter Carruthers: Olympic Pair Medalist & U.S. National Pair Champion with sister Kitty**

If you notice a lack of passion or motivation in your child, consider the cause as soon as you notice the change. Think back to your child's mission statement, as well as to the list of reasons most children participate in sports (fun being the number one reason) to help you discern what is missing. Is it due to pressure to succeed from you, the coach, or your child; boredom; lack of success, rest, or fun; overtraining; a deteriorating relationship with the coach; or too many injuries? Discuss with your child, the lead coach, and others in the Inner Champion Circle what can be done to support your child's efforts to get back in touch with the passion that was once there.

Lastly, make a mission statement for your own life. Live each day committed to making your mission a reality. Create goals that support your mission and the missions of you and your family, and rate your effort to achieve your goals each day. Be a role model by celebrating your successes and learning from your mistakes before moving on to your next set of goals.

Mental Toughness Training Exercises

Write a mission statement

1. Answer the following questions to discover more about yourself and what skating means to you. Write your answers in your mental toughness training journal.

   - Why do I skate? What do I love about it? Why did I start skating? Why did I keep skating?
   - What type of skater and person do I want to be?
   - What do I want to accomplish in skating? What is my greatest dream? What do I want to accomplish this year, in five years, and in ten years?
   - In addition to these accomplishments, what do I want to get out of skating? How can skating benefit my life now and years from now?
   - Which skaters do I admire and why? Which traits do they have that I want?
   - What do I want to be known for or remembered by? If my club held a party in my honor, what would I want them to celebrate? How do I want people to describe me as a skater and person?
   - What effect do I want to have on the people around me, an audience, and myself?
   - What brings me joy on the ice? What is fun? What is a challenge? What is exciting? What is satisfying? What makes me feel good?

2. Using your answers to the list of questions as a guide, select a clean sheet of paper in your journal and write a paragraph or short essay to explain why you skate, what you want to accomplish, what you want to get out of your skating experience, and what type of person and skater you want to be. What you write will be your mission statement for skating.

3. Post your mission statement in a place that will allow you to see it often, and be sure to read it if you feel discouraged, confused, exhausted, and overwhelmed.

4. Bring a copy of your mission statement with you to every event, and read it on the day of each performance.
5. Complete this mental toughness training exercise every year, because as you get older and more experienced, your mission may change.

Establish roles and responsibilities

This is an important exercise for all skaters and teams to complete. If you are a single skater, complete this exercise with the core members of your Inner Champion Circle. If you are part of a pair or dance team, complete this exercise with your partner and the core members of both of your Inner Champion Circles. If you are part of a large team, complete this exercise with all team members present before you complete the exercise with the core members of your Inner Champion Circle.

1. Identify everyone in your Inner Champion Circle. Remember that your circle can include many people, including coaches, on- and off-ice trainers, club and skating organization officials, sponsors, agents, parents, siblings, friends, spouses, arena management, and anyone else who contributes financially, emotionally, intellectually, or physically (either directly or indirectly) to your success.
2. Write a description of your role and responsibilities. Focus on what you and others in your circle can expect of you, as well as what should not be tolerated. If you are part of a team, describe the strengths you bring to the team, too. Ask the members of your circle and any team members to do the same.
3. Write a description of the roles and responsibilities of all the people in your Inner Champion Circle. Focus on what is expected of them, as well as what will not be tolerated. Include what they bring to the circle. Ask all the members of your circle and any team members to do the same.
4. Set up a meeting with the core members of your Inner Champion Circle and compare lists. If you are part of a team, do this step as a team. Next, check in with everyone in your Inner Champion Circle to compare lists. Make compromises if necessary. If a compromise is not possible,

either agree to disagree, or discuss and decide on how to make a change to your Inner Champion Circle.

Have a purpose

Follow the instructions below in the order listed. This exercise will illustrate the difference having a purpose makes when you are attempting something.

1. Stand up, cross your arms in front of you, and then open your arms and reach out to the side. At the same time, reach one leg off the ground and behind you. Do this ten times as fast as you can.
2. Jump up and land in a check-out position ten times as fast as you can.
3. Jump up as high as you can with a straight back and land in a check-out position with strength and control ten times as fast as you can. Do this while focusing on which muscles you are using to maintain control and correct posture.
4. Did you experience each item on the list differently? How? You probably noticed that you had no purpose or awareness while doing the first item, had a little bit of direction but still no purpose for the second item, and then had both an awareness and purpose for the last item. Which set of movements would have enabled you to hold on to the landing of your hardest jump?

Create a Star Map

A Star Map will help you decide on specific goals each year or season.

1. Draw a large star on a sheet of paper in your mental toughness training journal.
2. In the center of the star, write what your ultimate long-term goal is for the end of the competition season (or the end of the year if you are not competing).
3. On the outside lines of the star, write everything you will need to learn or improve to achieve your ultimate goal. Add extra lines if you need to. For example, you may want to go

to Sectionals or Nationals. Write this in the middle of the star. To accomplish this goal, you will have to pass certain tests and/or master certain jumps, combinations, spins, lifts, footwork, etc. You will also need to master your program(s) and improve certain mental skills. Be sure to include all aspects of skating, such as specific elements, presentation, endurance, and mental skills. Write all of these items on the lines of the star. As always, it is a good idea to talk with your coach and other members of your Inner Champion Circle while doing the various steps of goal setting.

4. Once you complete the star, rate the areas you need to improve in order of importance by writing 1 by the most important, 2 by the second most important, etc. (It is acceptable to tie items if they are equally important.)
5. On a new sheet of paper titled *My Goals for the Year 20XX* (fill in the numbers), list each item from your Star Map, with the most important at the top and the least important on the bottom. If they are all equally important, write them in any order.
6. Use a scale from 1 to 10 to rate how close you are in accomplishing each item by writing $X/10$ next to each line. For example, if you are really close to accomplishing an item, you would write 8/10 or 9/10. If you are just starting to learn an item, you would write 1/10 or 2/10.
7. You can now use this information to write SMART and Positive goals. Start with the most important, and use the 1-to-10 scale to decide how many steps you will need. Be sure to make a new star each year or season.

Set SMART and Positive goals

Create a section in your mental toughness training journal for your goals. Use one piece of paper for each goal. Make certain each goal is SMART and Positive, and be sure to discuss your goals with your coach and other members of your Inner Champion Circle.

1. At the top of the page, write one of your long-term goals from your Star Map exercise.

2. Write the completion date to the right of your goal.
3. Below the goal, write a positive statement about the goal as if you have already completed it. Imagine this affirmation each time you think of the goal.
4. Working your way down the paper and from the completion date to today's date, write as many short-term goals as you need. Write the target date to the right and an affirmation below each goal. If you have difficulty thinking of short-term goals, consider what you will have to do before the long-term goal is achievable.
5. Break your *steps* down into weekly or bi-weekly goals, depending on how far away your completion date is. If it is less than two weeks from the completion date, break your steps into daily goals.
6. Check the goal sheet at the end of each week to evaluate your progress. After you accomplish each step, reward yourself in some way, even if it is simply saying something encouraging to yourself.

Evaluate daily goals

Keeping track of daily goals can be a great confidence booster. Anytime you feel discouraged or you don't think you are improving, look at your daily goal sheets to remind yourself of how much you have accomplished. Make sure that all of your goals are SMART and Positive.

1. Put today's date on the first line of a sheet of paper. If you have already skated, write down tomorrow's date.
2. Write down your daily goals.
3. Look at this sheet at the end of the day and evaluate your success. What did you learn and accomplish? Rate your effort. Are you proud of what you did mentally and physically? What do you want to repeat, and what changes do you want to make for the next day?
4. Repeat this process each training day.
5. If you don't have time to complete this process in writing every day, create daily goals in your mind and evaluate your efforts before each training day is over. Before you step onto the ice each day, decide exactly what you want to

improve that day. Find the time to record at least a partial list of your daily successes as often as you can.

Make a daily evaluation chart

Create an evaluation chart for each program, dance, and/or moves in the field test you are working on this season. Include in your program chart a line for the date, all elements in your program, and a space to rate each element. You can use letter grades, a number scale, or plusses and minuses to rate your elements. The type of rating system is not important, but being consistent in how you rate yourself is. Make a chart for your moves test that includes all moves, and break dances into sections and areas of focus. Use this chart on each day you skate and use the feedback from the charts to guide your daily goal setting.

Use event goals

Complete this exercise at least one month before every event. Make sure all of your goals are SMART and Positive.

1. Write at least three goals in your journal before each event. Be certain to discuss these goals with your coach and others in your Inner Champion Circle to ensure everyone is working together.
2. Post affirmations for each of these goals. Imagine your affirmations each time you see them.
3. Focus on these goals as you prepare to perform.
4. Record in your journal how well you did after each event. Evaluate what you learned and accomplished. Celebrate your successes, learn from your mistakes, and move on to a higher level of skating.

Chapter 3

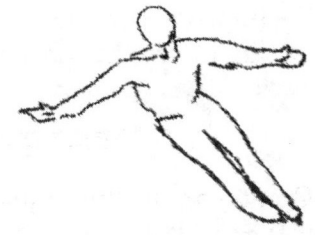

Think Like an Inner Champion

> *The only disability in life is a bad attitude.*
> **Scott Hamilton: Olympic, World & U.S. National Champion**

Negative Newt doesn't believe that controlling his thoughts or emotions is possible. This doesn't bother him very much because he also believes that what he thinks has little effect on his skating. He tries to be positive sometimes by thinking of corrections he has heard. For example, he thinks about not making mistakes, and as he skates into the hardest element in his program, he'll say to himself, *I hope I don't fall.* A lot of the time he does fall, so it makes him believe even more that his thoughts can't help him skate well.

Negative Newt also seems to dwell on the worst happening before every event, and this fills him with fear and self-doubt. He tries to push those thoughts out of his head, but he can't seem to stop thinking of all the things that could go wrong. It is easy for him to think of lots of different horrible possibilities because it seems like bad things always happen to him. In fact, as soon as he makes a mistake, he knows that it will be downhill from there, because he either gets frustrated or just sort of gives up. Either way, Negative Newt proves himself right as he makes mistake after mistake and ends up disappointed in his performance yet again.

Positive Polly figures she has the choice to fill her mind with positive thoughts that make her feel wonderful and confident or negative thoughts that make her feel bad and doubt herself. Her thoughts have helped her expect the best from herself even when things get tough, and she has found that what she expects is usually what she gets. She has learned that if she thinks of what she wants to do, instead of what not to do, she enjoys greater success.

Positive Polly has also noticed that she can look at the same situation in a variety of ways, and that each way makes her feel different. She now tries to look at things in a way that makes her feel the best possible. Her friends sometimes tease that she is always seeing the good in even the worst situation, but she doesn't mind the teasing because she seems happier, more successful, and better able to deal with difficult situations than most of her friends.

Confidence and the power of your thoughts

When athletes are asked to describe their best performance, they usually say something about having felt extremely confident before, during, and after their event. A big part of being confident is thinking you are able to do certain things. Self-confident athletes expect to do their best, and they usually do! Likewise, athletes who lack self-confidence usually doubt their abilities and rarely perform their best. If you don't think and believe you can do something, chances are you won't be successful (regardless of your physical strength and ability).

> *I cannot possibly overstate the importance of what an individual thinks and believes. . . . No matter what their skill level, their belief about themselves and their abilities is what will ultimately determine their level of success.*
> **Bernard Ford: World Dance Champion,**
> **Olympic & International Coach**

What you think and say to yourself can help or hurt your confidence and performance, even when you are not fully aware of what is going on in your head. Henry Ford once said, *Whether you think you can or think you can't, you're right.* Keep in mind what you learned in the first chapter about the mind-body connection – perceptions, thoughts, and the resulting emotions actually change the chemistry in the brain, and this change can affect a variety of performance factors, including coordination, balance, timing, energy level, and focus. Fortunately, you can learn to control what you think and say to yourself. This is called *self-talk control*, and it is a mental skill that you can learn to help improve your confidence. Self-talk control can also help you enhance your concentration, control your effort and mood, and speed up your ability to learn or improve skating elements.

Self-talk control

Think of your mind as a computer that you can program for success or failure through your self-talk. Negative, inappropriate, or too much self-talk can hurt your performance and therefore can be thought of as *stinking thinking*. However, the positive, appropriate self-talk of an Inner Champion can only enhance your performance. The key to confidence is to control your self-talk instead of letting your self-talk control you and your performance.

Before you can control your self-talk, you must be aware of it. You can increase your awareness by focusing on the things you say to yourself and your reaction to these thoughts while you practice. Try to remember the thoughts you had during recent tests and competitions, as well. Take the time to write a list of your thoughts and reactions in your mental toughness training journal, and you will probably notice a variety of things, from positive and negative thoughts in the form of simple words or phrases to long, drawn-out monologues. Try to identify any patterns with respect to which thoughts seem to help and which seem to hurt your performance.

Self-talk can be controlled by changing your perception, using a thought-stoppage technique, changing unwanted thoughts to positive, appropriate thoughts, countering negative thoughts, taking a time-out, using imagery, reframing irrational and distorted thinking, and creating affirmations.

This chapter explains how to do all of these things, and you will learn how self-talk control can be beneficial even beyond building confidence.

Change your perception

Chapter 1 explained how your perception of a situation affects your thoughts and emotions, as well as how your body responds. Emotions that bring out the best in a person include confidence, excitement, feeling challenged, and enjoyment. Emotions that bring out the worst in people include anger, fear, self-doubt, discouragement, and confusion. For example, when you perceive a situation as threatening or scary, you will have thoughts and emotions related to fear, doubt, and frustration. These thoughts and emotions can lead to your muscles tightening up and a change in your timing, neither of which will lead to a peak performance experience.

You can't always choose the details of the situation you are in, but you can choose your perception and your response. A situation in itself is not necessarily positive or negative, because feelings and emotions come from within; so choose your perception wisely. If you see a situation as threatening, decide to view it as a challenge that you can overcome, and calmly focus on the solution. You can also practice thinking of situations that normally seem scary or stressful as being exciting and fun.

> *If you have the proper perspective on competing, you will benefit. The whole process involves challenging yourself, believing in what you do, and overcoming any sense of doubt. That, to me, is what competition is really about.*
> **Michael Weiss: Olympian, World Medalist & U.S. National Champion**

Evaluate your perceptions to discover if you have formed bad habits in terms of how you perceive certain situations. Keep in mind that although there are many rules in skating, you will not find one rule stating a skater must be afraid and filled with stress when testing or competing. There is also no rule stating that once you make a mistake, the remainder of your performance must be a struggle. Even learning new elements can be viewed as fun, exciting, and something to be proud of instead of being stressful and frustrating. If you have developed some bad habits in how you see certain situations, practice looking at the same situations in a different, more helpful way.

> A wonderful example of how a change in perception can lead to great skating comes from **Paul Wylie**, U.S. Olympic Silver Medalist. At one time, he had difficulties with his triple axel combination. His problem did not stem from poor technique, but rather from his fear and dread of the element. Once he realized the root of his problem, he decided to view the element in a different way. He thought about how much people would pay to experience the same sensations as he did when he completed the combination. He figured that if Disneyland had a ride that could provide a similar experience, people would be willing to stand in long lines and pay big bucks for such a fun and exciting opportunity. Once he got over his fear by changing his perception, he had greater success with the element in competitions, and he even started to enjoy doing it!

The next time you are experiencing stinking thinking and negative emotions, check in with your perception of the situation. Figure out how to change it to bring about better thoughts, emotions, and behaviors. If you normally feel defeated, doubtful, or otherwise negative as soon as you are faced with a seemingly difficult situation, your perception and negative reaction is a bad habit that can be changed with some effort on your part. Remember that you choose how you view the world around you! Choose to respond to challenges with positive thoughts that focus on solutions and what you can control at that moment.

> *I started to lose perspective. I felt like I didn't love skating as much, and I was always thinking negative thoughts like, "What if I don't win?"*
> **Michelle Kwan: most decorated U.S. female skater, describing a disappointing season**

Use thought stoppage

To use this technique, you must first become aware of your thinking and the effect it has on your ability to perform. Use the *self-talk log* exercises at the end of this chapter to identify helpful Inner Champion thoughts and the stinking thinking you should stop. Pay attention to your thoughts and notice which ones are encouraging or discouraging, which bring out the best you have to offer or distract you, which are energizing or draining, and which pump you up or bring you down. Thoughts that are negative, irrational, overly analytical, pressuring, irrelevant to what you are doing at the moment, or that you would feel bad about saying to your best friend are stinking thinking.

After becoming aware of your thoughts, the next step is to stop stinking thinking. To do this, you need to briefly focus on the thought and then use a trigger of your choice to stop the thought. The trigger can be thinking or saying *stop, delete, quiet, shut-up,* or *flush* (as in down the toilet the thought goes); picturing a stop sign; squeezing your hand; picturing the color red; picturing a police officer, palm out, standing in front of you; and so on. You can pick any trigger you want, as long as it sends the message to your brain to **STOP** those unwanted thoughts! Just remember that eliminating stinking thinking is like changing any bad habit. It will take time, effort, and practice.

You can practice thought stoppage off ice by imagining yourself in a situation in which stinking thinking usually occurs. Let the unwanted thoughts come to mind, then practice using your trigger to stop your stinking thinking. When deciding which thoughts are appropriate, *be your own best friend.* In other words, if you are not sure if your thoughts are overly critical or harsh, ask yourself if you would be willing to say the same thing about your best skating friend to his or her face. If you would feel uncomfortable saying something to your friend, you shouldn't say it to yourself. It is unfortunate that some people treat themselves with great disrespect and are downright mean in the way they talk to themselves. Yet most of these people would never consider saying the same sort of things to someone they didn't like, let alone their best friend. To bring out the best you have to offer, make an effort to be your own best friend at all times. This is especially important when you are feeling frustrated, scared, or otherwise negative.

Change stinking thinking to Inner Champion thoughts

In addition to stopping stinking thinking, you need to replace it with Inner Champion thoughts that provide encouragement and/or direct your attention properly. This mental skill is effective because it is impossible to give equal attention to two different thoughts at the same time. In changing unwanted thoughts, you take control of your self-talk by deciding what to think about. The new thoughts should be positive, simple, and in the present, and they should bring your focus back to what you can control in the situation. For example, stop and change, *I can't believe I just fell on that jump; the judges will mark me down for certain*, to, *I will land this next jump by doing a good set-up and check-out*.

Your replacement thoughts should also be realistic and focus on what you want to do instead of what you want to avoid, just like goals. For example, stop and replace *Since I just fell, I hope I don't fall on the next jump* with *I will perform this next jump just like I usually do*. If your coach gives you corrections in terms of what not to do, change the corrections in your mind to think about what you want to do. For example, if you are told to stop bending over when stroking, think of maintaining a strong core and correct posture instead. If you are unsure of how to change a correction into positive terms, be sure to ask your coach what you should be trying to do.

> Many top athletes rely on a form of this technique to control their self-talk. Once when Olympic Champion **Brian Boitano** was waiting between his warm-up and performance, he kept worrying about his triple lutz. Even though the jump was very consistent, he kept thinking repeatedly, *What if I miss my lutz?* Brian calls that little negative voice in his head *Murphy*, after Murphy's Law, which says whatever can go wrong, will go wrong. When it was time for Brian to perform, it didn't surprise him when he missed

the lutz. After that disappointing experience, he was determined that he would never again ask himself, *What if?* Instead, he decided that he would fill his mind with thoughts about how to do each element correctly. If Murphy's negativity did pop up in his mind, he just replaced each negative thought with a positive statement about his technique. Brian went on to become one of the most consistent skaters in skating history. This is an excellent example of how a true Inner Champion learned to control his thoughts.

Thought-stoppage is an important self-talk control technique because it is not realistic to expect yourself to be able to eliminate all stinking thinking, but you can always stop and replace unwanted thoughts with self-enhancing thoughts. It may be helpful to take one or two deep breaths between noticing stinking thinking and changing it to an Inner Champion thought. Imagine breathing away the unwanted thought before you think of the new, improved thought. You can also use the various imageries described later in this chapter to help you stop and change your unwanted thoughts.

It will be extremely beneficial to complete the exercise at the end of this chapter called *Change stinking thinking to Inner Champion thoughts* while you learn to stop and change unwanted thoughts. Also, practice this technique off the ice by imagining yourself skating. Let unwanted thoughts enter your mind, and then use your trigger to stop the thoughts and replace them with positive thoughts. When this becomes easy, try it on the ice. The last step is using this technique during an event.

Counter persistent stinking thinking

Sometimes when you stop and replace stinking thinking, you might find that you don't believe the replacement thought or that the old thought keeps popping back into your mind. If this happens, first make sure the new thought is realistic and based on your true abilities. If it isn't, change the new thought to one that is more appropriate. If the new thought is realistic and your perception is desirable, use *countering*, which is like being an investigator or your own lawyer.

Countering consists of finding evidence for why the new thought is correct and why you are wrong to disbelieve it. For example, if you think, *I'll never be able to skate a clean program,* and then you change that to, *I can skate a clean program and I will* – but you don't believe it – use countering. First focus on the reasons why you believe the unwanted thought and think of any facts that prove those reasons to be untrue. Then look at the facts that prove the positive thought is true. In the case of skating a clean program, remind yourself of the facts that you can land everything in the program when you warm up, that you have mastered other programs before, that you have been working on building up your endurance, and so on. Find the facts and make a convincing argument to yourself.

Take a time-out to be negative

Sometimes you might find that even countering does not change your stinking thinking. You may feel extremely down on yourself or you may be having a horrible day when everything seems to go against you. If you find yourself in such a situation, try taking a time-out to be negative on purpose (only as a last resort).

Step off the ice (or face the railing) if you are on the ice when you need a time-out. Give yourself a time limit of no longer than three minutes, and let yourself think of as many negative thoughts as possible. Allow your body and emotions to experience the negativity as well. When your time is up, take a deep breath and get back on the ice (or turn away from the railing) with a new, positive attitude. Change your perception, fill your mind with Inner Champion thoughts, and get to work!

Imagine your stinking thinking away

Use your imagination to get rid of stinking thinking by trying the various suggestions described in this section. You can also think of your own imageries – just be creative and make it fun. Always finish by thinking of thoughts that are positive, simple, under your control, and in the present.

The Sweep. Sweep your mind clean of stinking thinking by imagining you have an internal sweep or vacuum to rid your mind of unwanted thoughts.

Computer Virus. Imagine your mind is like a computer that can be programmed for success or failure. Scan your mind to check for viruses (stinking thinking) and then delete, eject, or dump any viruses that you find. Follow up by running the Inner Champion thought program.

Wipe Your Blades and Mind Clean. If you are feeling negative and defeated, wipe the snow off your blades and imagine wiping your mind clean at the same time. Throw the snow over the railing or off to the side as you imagine throwing away your stinking thinking.

Land Mines. Imagine unwanted thoughts are like land mines that need to be disposed of immediately upon discovery. Blow them up, throw them away, or do anything you can imagine to get rid of them.

Fuel Your Mind. Your mind, just like your body and car, needs proper fuel to function at a high level. Imagine that the thoughts in your mind are like food at a buffet counter. Fill your mind up with only Inner Champion thoughts, and leave the rest behind.

The Flush. Flush any stinking thinking down, down, and away out of your mind.

Blow It Off. Use your breath to get rid of stinking thinking. As you breathe out, imagine all of your stinking thinking being carried away by the air you exhale. As you breathe in, imagine filling yourself up with Inner Champion thoughts and feelings.

Shake It Off. Shake your hands or head and imagine shaking any stinking thinking away from your mind and body. (Of course, don't use this imagery at a time that can interrupt your skating.)

The Garden. Imagine that your mind is like a garden. All your positive, helpful thoughts are like flowers that need to be attended to and nurtured. The blooms of great thoughts are great performances. Plant Inner Champion thoughts in your mind, and pay attention to them to keep them strong and able to bloom. All gardens have weeds, and in your mind weeds are stinking thinking. Get rid of unwanted thoughts by pulling them out of your mind's garden and tossing them away.

The Ocean. Imagine you are floating in the ocean and your thoughts are things that are floating around you. Decide what thoughts you want to simply let float away by not paying any attention to them and what thoughts you want to grab on to in order to keep you afloat or soar away to the land of Inner Champions.

Computer Game. Imagine that your thoughts are on a computer game screen. Zap the ones you don't want and capture the ones you need.

Get Lost! Imagine your stinking thinking as being the voice of your worst enemy, an overly critical coach, a little devil, the world's biggest pessimist Murphy, or Stinker, the master of stinking thinking. Each time you have unwanted thoughts, tell the imaginary person to get lost, and then replace the thoughts with a statement that you would hear from your best friend, your dream coach, a little angel, or the most optimistic person you can think of.

Play the Role of an Inner Champion. The next time you find yourself feeling negative or in a seemingly impossible situation, think of how your favorite skater, athlete, or person would deal with the situation. Imagine how he or she would act, think, and behave, and then imagine you are just like that person and do the same thing. If you don't have a favorite person that you look up to, imagine what you would do at your best, and then go do it!

Change irrational and distorted thoughts

Certain types of thoughts can be detrimental to confidence even though they might not seem negative. These thoughts should be changed, too. All these types of thoughts can be dealt with using the various self-talk control techniques. Following are descriptions of the most common irrational and distorted thoughts:

Perfection is essential. Striving to be your best has great value and can be motivating, but demanding perfection is unrealistic and destructive to your self-confidence and performance. No human is perfect, not even you! You must make mistakes in order to learn and improve. Think of mistakes and failures as opportunities to learn, grow, and develop in your quest to be the best you can be. Accepting mistakes as part of the sport allows you to stop worrying about being perfect and frees your mind to allow the best you have to offer to surface. Replace your desire to be perfect with the desire to give full effort to what you are doing at the moment.

> *I knew right when I stepped on the ice that I wasn't going to worry about anything. I was going to enjoy the moment. . . . I didn't skate for anything like a perfect program. . . . I went out with a great attitude, and I innately knew it was going to be a great program.*
> **Sarah Hughes: Olympic Champion, World & U.S. National Medalist, describing her Olympic-winning freeskate**

The next time you put pressure on yourself to be absolutely perfect, take the perfection test. Start the test by filling a tub with six inches of water. If you don't have a tub available, use the steps in a pool, a large pan that you can step into, or even a puddle. Next, take off your shoes and socks, roll up your pants, and step into the water. If your feet float on top of the water without touching the bottom, you are perfect and should expect perfection in everything you do. However, if your feet touch the bottom of the tub (or whatever you are using), you did not pass the perfection test and therefore can't logically demand perfection from yourself. If this happens, accept that you are a mere mortal like everyone else and that you will make mistakes along the way in your life's journey. Just be sure to learn from every mistake to get the most possible out of the opportunity mistakes present.

Catastrophizing. This is when you constantly ask, *What if something bad happens?* Although it is good to be prepared for a variety of situations, there is a big difference between constantly worrying about or expecting the worst to happen and being prepared for the worst. This thought process is mentally and physically draining, unrealistic, and a waste of time because you can't control the future. When thinking about the future, get in the habit of considering how wonderful it would be if the best happens. Live by the principle *Be prepared for the worst but expect the best.*

My worth depends on my achievements. You must remember that your worth as a person is based on many other things besides what you accomplish as an athlete! Skating is something that you do, and it is not what you are. A performance will not make or break who you are as a person, and the sun will always come up tomorrow no matter how great or how poorly you skate. Keeping skating in perspective will take a lot of pressure off you to perform, and you will in turn be free to perform your best.

Extreme thinking. Thinking that is extreme in nature includes such words as *always* and *never* and is usually inaccurate. For example, thinking that you always skate badly on a certain day, at a certain time, or at a certain rink is extreme thinking that will only place limits on what you can do. If you start to believe these thoughts, you will find a way to make yourself correct. Be sure your thoughts are setting you up for success and not failure!

Use self-talk control for more than confidence

Self-talk control can be used for learning new skills, changing bad habits, controlling your attention, creating your mood, and controlling your effort.

Learning new skills. When you first learn a skill, instructional self-talk is helpful. This self-talk should be kept as simple as possible to avoid *paralysis by analysis* – overloading the mind-body connection by thinking too much! Try to focus on only one or two things at a time. As you master skills, the talk should become shorter and less frequent, and, if comfortable for you, the focus can change from technical cues to optimal feelings and timing.

Changing bad habits. Instructional self-talk can be used to change a bad habit that is part of a well-learned skill. This talk should be detailed at first and focus on what you want to do instead of what you want to avoid. For example, *Keep straight* instead of *Don't lean over*. As with new skills, the goal is to relearn the skill and eventually minimize the self-talk.

Attentional focus control. You can direct your attention back to the present when you are distracted or find yourself wandering to the past (for example, thinking, *If only I'd done that first combo*) or the future (thinking, *I'd better not fall on that combo in the last section*, while skating the middle section). Use a cue word or positive statement concerning the element you are doing or about to do.

Creating your mood. By thinking simple cue words, you can have an effect on your emotions, mood, and movement to help you interpret your music. For example, use cue words such as *intense and strong* at the start of your last section, or *slow, soft,* and *smooth* during slow music. Depending on what the music calls for, you can use other cue words such as *happy feet, flirty, salsa, drama queen* or *king,* or whatever adjective works to help you create the appropriate mood.

Controlling your effort. Energy and persistence can be maintained, in part, by self-talk. Use self-talk for motivation in the morning, to combat boredom or fatigue during practice, and to fight pain. Cue words such as *explode, pick it up, go for it, bring it on,* and *attack* can work for this purpose.

Increase confidence with additional methods

Although self-talk control is highly effective, you can improve your confidence by using a variety of other methods in combination with the self-talk control techniques.

Create affirmations. Your affirmations should be statements about yourself that are based on goals, past successes, and positive qualities. You can increase your confidence and keep your perspective in check and your thoughts positive by creating affirmations and focusing on them throughout the day. Affirmations build your confidence by drawing your attention to all the reasons you can trust and believe in yourself, your technique, your preparation, your determination, and your training.

Affirmations should be positive, action-oriented self-statements such as *I jump well in my program,* instead of *I know I can jump well in my program.* Affirmations should not be in perfectionist terms, such as *I always . . . ,* or *I never . . . ,* because nobody is perfect! Follow the affirmation exercise at the end of this chapter to help you write your affirmations in your journal, and use sticky notes to post them in your bedroom, bathroom, car, etc.

Create as many affirmations as you can and add to the list every day. Focus on these statements before and during events, before you sleep, when you wake up – all the time! Before an event, post as many affirmations as you can all around your environment. The objective when creating affirmations is not to be modest, but to be honest. If it feels like you are bragging when you do this exercise, remind yourself that these statements are only for you to read and think about. You don't need to share them with anyone (except maybe a hotel maid!).

Are you filling yourself up with put-ups or put-downs?
Kathy Casey: Olympic, World & National Coach

If you are part of a team, use teamwork to create team affirmations in addition to having affirmations you create alone. Team affirmations are useful for building team spirit and enhancing team cohesion. If you find that your partner or a team member is feeling negative, remind the person of a team affirmation to help him or her regain positive focus and think more like an Inner Champion.

Act like an Inner Champion. Your body language (your posture, facial expression, and movements) can have a dramatic impact on your level of confidence. Act self-assured – even when you are filled with self-doubt – to feel and perform with confidence. The next time you experience fear, frustration, or doubt, hold your head high, skate with commanding posture, and use your face to express joy and assuredness in what you are doing. Chances are that if you act as though you are confident and having fun, your mind will soon start to believe your body, and the end result will be feeling, and skating with, confidence.

Remind yourself as often as possible to act how you want to feel and think. During practice ice and warm-up ice at events, present yourself in a calm, poised, focused, brave, and confident manner. If you make a mistake, shake it off with a smile, knowing you will be able to correct it next time. You need to think it, believe it, act it, and do it.

Be prepared and have trust. You can enhance your confidence level by being properly prepared and having trust in yourself, your training, and your Inner Champion Circle. The more prepared you are, the more you will feel ready and able to meet any challenge that comes your way. Work hard to master proper technique, train consistently, and treat every practice like it is a performance. Each clean performance run-through will strengthen the trust and confidence you have in yourself.

> *My hard work paid off at competition. I felt confident waiting to perform, knowing that I had done everything I could to prepare myself. My confidence made it easy to skate with determination instead of just hoping it would happen.*
>
> **Elaine Zayak: Olympian, World & U.S. National Champion**

It is equally important that you trust the knowledge of your coaches and others guiding your skating career. If you take the time to develop a good working relationship with the people in your Inner Champion Circle, you will find it easier to have trust in them. Being prepared and having trust in yourself and your Inner Champion Circle will allow you to free your mind and let your body do what it has been trained to do.

Experience success. Being successful is yet another way a person can boost his or her confidence level. Setting and achieving daily, weekly, and monthly goals will allow you to experience an abundance of success. Doing imageries of skating your best and completing difficult elements will also have a positive impact on your confidence.

Spend time with other Inner Champions. The people you choose to spend time with can make it easier or harder for you to bring out your best. Surround yourself with optimistic people who act and think like an Inner Champion as much as possible.

Is it possible to be too confident?

It is not possible to be too confident! Confidence is a feeling that is based on facts and true abilities. As long as your opinion of yourself is honest, you will have no problems. However, it is possible to have an inflated sense of self-importance that can have a negative effect on your training and performance. This happens when people's opinions of themselves and their abilities are not based on facts and reality. A person with a big head might become lazy in training or hold back at a competition, which could produce disastrous results. No one is so good, strong, or talented that she doesn't need to train or put her best effort into a performance. Just be honest!

Self-talk control, confidence, and life

Be certain to remember that self-talk control, like other mental skills, can be used in all areas of your life. Self-talk control can be used to improve your overall confidence and to change any thoughts that are not having a beneficial effect on your well-being. Anytime you are feeling discouraged about something, check your thoughts and decide if your perception and thoughts should be changed. Follow the same steps as you would with your thoughts about skating.

Creating affirmations about aspects other than skating can also have a positive influence on the quality of your life. You can post these affirmations on sticky notes as you do with your skating affirmations. Another helpful idea is to be aware of how you ask people to do things. Try to ask for what you want instead of what you don't want. For example, instead of telling someone, *Don't forget . . .* and *Don't do . . .* , it is better to say, *Please remember . . .* and *Please do . . .*

Self-talk control: final round

As an Inner Champion, decide how to perceive the world around you. Recognize that what you think and ultimately how you respond in a situation is your responsibility if you want the best from yourself. Accept this responsibility and make sure you choose wisely. Pump yourself up instead of putting yourself down. Don't just think you can do something, but imagine it happening, believe it is possible, and act like you can do it. A situation or past experience can't determine what you think, because only you control your thoughts. Even in tough situations, choose to keep things in perspective and think simple, positive thoughts about what you can control.

Look for the best in each situation, and accept that mistakes are part of the learning process. Make sure to train smart and be well prepared for each event. Make an effort to be your own best friend by trusting and believing in yourself, your training and preparation, your toughness, and your ability to face anything that comes your way. When you expect your best, feel prepared, and free your mind from worry, you can just let your body do what it has been trained to do. Doubt your doubts, not yourself. After all, if you can't trust and believe in yourself, whom or what can you trust and believe in?

Following this advice will help you feel confident about being able to handle any situation the best you can at that moment. Now that you know how, make a commitment that beginning today you will walk the walk, talk the talk, think the thoughts, and see the world like an Inner Champion and skate great!

Message to coaches and parents

Coaches:

Think about what types of thoughts help bring out the best you have to offer. Which thoughts undermine your performance as a coach? Which thoughts help you be the most effective you can be? Is it different during practice and competition, work and play, or at home and at the rink? Are you an optimist or a pessimist? Keep in mind that you are a role model, so using a positive, controlled approach in coaching, especially in stressful situations, is a powerful tool for both you and your students.

> *A coach has got to be a role model. I think that's extremely essential because the years we're training them are their growing years, where they're developing as people as well as skaters.*
> **Ron Ludington: Olympic Medalist & Olympic, World & National Coach**

Take the time to determine how you can help each of your students become and remain confident. Encourage optimism in your students by being optimistic yourself. Check in with how your students are perceiving situations, and point out better viewpoints when they are not seeing things in the best light. Further reinforce a positive perspective by pointing out what you thought your students did well, what improved, or what they learned at the end of each lesson. Ask your students to use your lesson review and their own ideas to maintain a list of affirmations that reflect what they liked about themselves each day. Knowing that they have a list to add to will help your students to look for their positive qualities.

People usually get what they expect, so avoid placing limits on your students. Expect the best from them, and ask that they expect the best from themselves, too. Given that confidence, or lack of, can be catching and that you are a role model, make a habit of expecting the best from yourself, as well. Displaying confidence in yourself will help your students trust you, your guidance and instruction, their technique, and their training. Expressing confidence in your students' abilities will further enhance their trust in themselves.

Your method of instruction can have a great impact on the type of thoughts your students have while skating. Give positive feedback to your students as much as possible, and state corrections and evaluations in a way that will best help your students believe that they can do what you ask them to do. Sandwich corrections within positive feedback as often as you can, and state your requests in simple terms of what you want instead of what you don't want. Focus on strengths immediately before and during events, because then it is too late to change weaknesses, and try your best to sandwich evaluation information by starting and finishing with positives after each performance. This may be difficult to do after poor performances, but keep it simple by pointing out that they showed up, kept going, held their head high at the end, etc.

> *When teaching an element, you have to balance demanding specific positions with encouragement, and always recognize effort in the learning process.*
> **Tom Zakrajsek: International & National Coach**

To enhance your confidence and perspective on life, create your own personal affirmation list, and add five items to the list on a daily basis. You might be pleasantly surprised with how your perception changes when you know you will need to come up with five positives about yourself at the end of the day; chances are you will start to focus more on what is good about you and your day. Apply your favorite self-talk control techniques to your life, as well.

Parents:

When your child is an athlete, one of the most important aspects of your parental role is to be your child's biggest fan. However, if you are caught up in the role of instructing and critiquing your child's skating, the positive impact you can have as a parent will be greatly diminished. You already pay a coach to instruct and give critiques, so stay focused on taking every opportunity to express your belief in your child's abilities. It also critical for your child to understand that your love will not change, regardless of how he or she skates and performs.

Make a special effort to stress your child's strengths before and during events without getting overly technical. This can be significant to your child's confidence level because at that point it is too late to make improvements, and your child is usually all too aware of his or her weaknesses. Encourage your child to maintain an optimistic perspective, and to think and talk about himself or herself in a self-appreciating manner. Pump up your child as much as possible by pointing out his or her positive qualities as often as you can. A person cannot be over confident if his or her beliefs are based on facts! The power of a parent believing in a child is immense; make sure your child knows you have unwavering confidence in his or her abilities.

> *The coaches teach and prepare the skater for special events – [parents] encourage! That is the number one job of the parent. Find one thing positive to say at the end of each day [and] your rewards will be beyond belief.*
> **B. L. Wylie: Mother of Olympic Medalist Paul Wylie**

Encourage your child to spend time with optimistic people as opposed to people who put themselves or others down most of the time. Be a role model by keeping an optimistic perspective and expressing great thoughts about yourself. Talk about solutions more than problems, and approach difficult situations as challenges that can be overcome instead of obstacles that can hold you back.

Mental Toughness Training Exercises

Start a self-talk log for training

Fold a blank page in your mental toughness training journal in half length-wise to form two columns. Title the page *Self-talk Log for Training,* and label the left column *Perception & Thoughts* and the right column *Effect on Emotions and Performance.* Throughout one week, increase your awareness of your perception and the thoughts you have while training. Ask yourself if how you perceived situations and what you thought about yourself each day was encouraging and helpful to your confidence level or discouraging, distracting, draining, etc. Use this sheet to record your perceptions and thoughts, and the effect they had on your emotions and performance. Try to notice any patterns in terms of which thoughts seem to help and which seem to hurt your performance.

Keep a self-talk log for events

Fold a blank page in your mental toughness training journal in half length-wise to form two columns. Title the page *Self-talk Log for Events,* and label the left column *Perceptions & Thoughts* and the right column *Effect on Emotions and Performance.* Imagine being at your most recent event and focus on your perceptions, thoughts, emotions, and performance. Use this sheet to record your perceptions, thoughts, and your reactions. Try to notice any patterns in terms of which thoughts seem to help and which seem to hurt your performance.

Change stinking thinking to Inner Champion thoughts

Fold a blank page in your mental toughness training journal in half length-wise to form two columns. Title the page *Changing Thoughts,* and label the left column *Stinking Thinking* and the right column *Inner Champion Thoughts.* Make a third column between them on the crease of the paper, and label it *Trigger.*

In the *Stinking Thinking* column, list the thoughts from training and events that do not have a positive effect on you and your performance. After each item in the first column, use the center column to write the trigger you will use to stop the stinking thinking. Lastly, use the *Inner Champion Thoughts* column to list each replacement thought. Make sure the new thoughts are simple, realistic, and focus on what you want to do, and that they are under your control. Go over this sheet often until the positive thoughts come to your mind easily.

Following are examples of replacement thoughts:
- *I am so tired that I can just fall over* can be changed to, *Just do it! If I can do it now, I know I can do it anytime, anywhere, no matter what.*
- *Quit bending over* can be changed to *Stand up straight.*
- *This is too hard and I should just quit* can be changed to, *Stay tough and I will triumph over this bump in the road. It's not over until it's over!*
- *Don't drop your left side* can be changed to *Keep your left side up* or *Stay even.*
- *Oh my gosh, I can't believe I just did that. How embarrassing,* can be changed to, *That must have looked kind of funny. Oh well, time to move on* (and laugh it off).
- *Don't slow down* can be changed to *Stay strong and push hard.*
- *Everything that can go wrong is going wrong. I should just give up,* can be changed to, *I like challenges because I can handle anything. Bring it on strong because I am even stronger! Make it tough because I am even tougher.*
- *I can't breathe* can be changed to *Take slow, deep, even ribcage breaths and I will be fine.*
- *This is scary and I am afraid* can be changed to, *I love this challenge. I am going to feel great when I get it. I can always figure out how to be my best.*
- *I am out of energy and I don't think I can finish* can be changed to, *I am tougher than this! Go attack.*
- *I am so stiff I can't move* can be changed to *Let go and get into the flow.*

- *Oh no, the moment of truth is here* can be changed to *I trust my training.*
- *I hope I am ready for this* can be changed to *I'm ready so bring it on!*

Imagine stinking thinking away

Try the suggested imageries from this chapter to practice getting rid of unwanted thoughts. Always finish by thinking an Inner Champion thought. After trying them all out, decide which ones work the best for you and keep using them. Be creative and come up with your own imageries as well; just make them quick and fun. Keep track of which imageries work the best for you in your journal.

Create affirmations

Start an affirmation list in your mental toughness training journal and create as many affirmations about yourself as you can. Use affirmations based on your past successes, your current goals, the positive thoughts from your *Change stinking thinking to Inner Champion thoughts* exercise, and all of the good qualities that you possess. Include statements regarding why you can trust and believe in yourself, your training, and your preparation. Once you have started your affirmation list, add to the list on a daily basis. Every day, write three to five things that you accomplished or liked about yourself. This process will train your mind to look for the good in every situation and help you maintain the perception of an Inner Champion.

Use sticky notes to post affirmations from your list all around your environment. Post them in your hotel room when you travel to events. When you read or think of the affirmations, try to imagine and feel what the affirmations say. In other words, experience the affirmation each time you read it!

Use confident body language

1. Sit in a chair and slump as much as you can. Frown your best frown, let your eyes drop down, and let your body go limp. How do you feel? Stay in that position and think of some stinking thinking you have had recently about yourself or some non-constructive criticism that has been directed to you. How easy is it to believe these things when you sit there in a slump?
2. Sit tall, smile, look up and out at the world around you, and feel the strength in your muscles as you sit with great posture. Now how do you feel? Think of the same stinking thinking or non-constructive criticism. You will probably notice that these things are easier to dismiss when your body language is more confident. Keep this exercise in mind the next time you need a boost in confidence, and use your body language to your advantage. Remember to walk the walk, talk the talk, think the thoughts, and see the world like an Inner Champion to feel and skate great!

Some athletes find that concentrating on a graphic pattern or design helps them block out distractions. Want to try?

Focus on the design below as you repeat the following affirmation (or repeat an affirmation of your choosing).

I trust my training and I believe in myself.

Chapter 4

To Relax or Energize? That Is the Question.

> *The Olympics are pretty stressful and I think I relaxed a little bit and just let myself have fun. I think it worked.*
> **Tara Lipinski: Olympic, World & U.S. National Champion**

Negative Nettie gets extremely nervous when she competes. When she complained about it to her parents, they told her to just relax and have fun when she performs. The only problem is that she doesn't know how to relax. Before the warm-up at her last competition, she told her coach about how nervous she felt, and he told her to take some breaths and calm down. She tried this, but she took too many quick breaths and became light-headed. After the warm-up, her coach gave her a pep talk, but that made her feel even more uptight.

Negative Nettie's hands get clammy, her asthma acts up, and she can't seem to feel her legs when she gets really nervous. The more she tries to get into the ice, the stiffer she feels. To make matters worse, she rarely sleeps the night prior to an event, so her mind and body always feel tired even before she gets to the rink to perform. Sometimes Negative Nettie gets so nervous that she feels sick to her stomach and she just wants to cry or withdraw from the competition.

Positive Pete used to get really tired during practice. Part of the problem was that he had a hard time falling asleep at night. He also found that the more he thought about how tired he was, the worse he felt. Positive Pete's coach noticed his lack of energy in the morning. The coach told Pete that he would feel more motivated if before each practice he focused on what he wanted to accomplish and how great it would feel to be successful, instead of thinking about how tired he felt. His coach also suggested that he try to get more sleep and eat better to be properly rested and fueled for his training sessions.

Positive Pete also asked his older sister, an elite track athlete, if she had any ideas for him, and she taught him how she relaxed her mind and body at night to fall asleep right away. He followed the advice of both his coach and his sister, and he found that his energy level was much higher during training sessions. With increased energy, Positive Pete was able to get a lot more of his goals accomplished.

Not everyone is the same

Each person has a certain level of *activation*, or amount of mental and physical energy, that he or she needs to perform at his or her best. Some people need to be very relaxed, while others need to be extremely energized. Activation levels often change in response to a situation or stressor, such as negative thoughts before competing, fear of failing, skating several events in one day, or getting psyched out by competitors. Most problems arise when athletes are over-activated, such as when skaters get nervous about competing and their muscles become so tight that they can't skate up to their potential. Skaters can also be under-activated (although this is more common in practice than during competition), which results in being too relaxed or tired to skate well.

Fortunately, you can learn how to control your activation level. This chapter covers several different ways to relax and energize yourself. However, you must first discover more about your optimal level of activation. It is also important to be able to identify the *stressors* (things that cause you stress) and *energy zappers* (things that drain your energy) that commonly interfere with your activation level.

Optimal activation level

Think back to one of your great performances and focus on how relaxed, excited, energized, or mellow you were. What was your activation level? How did you feel physically? How did you feel mentally? It is important to be aware of which activation level works best for you, so you can know when to make an adjustment and whether you need to be more energized or relaxed.

Now think back to your most recent poor performance. What do you remember about the experience? Were you energized to the point of being so hyper that you couldn't stay focused? Were you constantly getting distracted? Or were you too relaxed, seemingly without the energy or strength to get through the event? What was it like? What did your body feel like? What was going on in your mind? What was it about the situation that caused you to react this way? Complete the exercises at the end of this chapter to find out more about your optimal activation level, what usually causes you stress or zaps your energy, and how you react to these stressors and energy zappers.

Fight or flight response

If you have ever been over-activated by stressors and skated poorly as a result, some things you might remember are that your muscles felt too tight or heavy to work properly, or that your muscles were so rubber-like that you couldn't get control of your body. Other common sensations are having butterflies, having sweaty palms, breathing in a fast, shallow manner, feeling nauseous, having a pounding heart, and shaking all over. Mentally you might have felt afraid, experienced a lot of negative thoughts, or felt as though time was sped up or like you couldn't stay focused on one thing for very long.

Most of these sensations are the result of the *fight or flight response,* which is a primitive physiological survival mechanism. When humans feel threatened, fearful, or severely nervous, their brains and bodies naturally respond by releasing chemicals. These chemicals affect mental and physical behavior in a way that originally evolved to help them either fight or escape the threat or source of fear and nervousness.

Unfortunately for skating, the results of this survival mechanism usually hinder performance, because the response is often too extreme. However, you can learn to control the intensity of this response by confronting such situations with calmness, courage, and confidence. As a result of this control, you can perceive the situation as a welcomed challenge you can handle and interpret your feelings as a sign that you are ready to perform. This will enable you to enjoy the challenges you face and use the extra energy to enhance your performance.

> Everyone gets nervous. It's natural, it's good. With nervousness comes adrenaline. . . . [Use] relaxation techniques . . . to help your mind and body regulate your nerves.
> **Paul Wylie: Olympic & U.S. National Medalist**

It will be beneficial for you to identify situations that commonly cause you stress. By doing so, you can prepare yourself for these situations ahead of time. It is also important that you increase your awareness of how you usually respond to these potential stressors. With this awareness, you will be able to recognize when your activation level is changing and quickly take control of your mind, body, and performance.

Relaxation

There are several relaxation techniques you can use when you are faced with stressors or just want to feel more relaxed. Your choice will depend on whether you want *complete relaxation* to sleep or cool down after skating or *alert relaxation* for when you are on the ice or getting ready to skate. How you respond to each technique will also help you determine which techniques suit you best. Just remember to give each technique a chance to develop before you decide which ones will work for you.

Breathing techniques. Deep *ribcage breathing* is the simplest and quickest relaxation technique. Ribcage breathing can be used for both alert and complete relaxation. Unlike other deep-breathing techniques, ribcage breathing allows you to take full breaths while maintaining your core strength. Ribcage breathing is relaxing for several reasons. The rhythm of ribcage breathing is calming, and it brings your focus to the present moment. Focused ribcage breathing can help you release unwanted thoughts, feelings, and distractions, and in slowing down your breathing, you can improve your performance by increasing the amount of oxygen in your blood stream. (Muscles require oxygen to function.) It also changes your focus from whatever is over-activating you to something you can control (your breathing and your body).

Circular ribcage breathing. Let your ribcage expand with air while you breathe in through your nose, and then keep your ribcage as wide as you can while you breathe out through your mouth. Imagine your breath moving in a circular motion as it enters through your nose, expands your ribcage, and exits through your mouth. It is important to maintain proper posture while breathing by keeping your shoulders down (keep the space between your ears and shoulders as wide as you can) and the core area of your body stable.

Ribcage breathing is most relaxing when you establish an even rhythm. Count to three as you breathe in, pause a moment, and count to four as you breathe out. Try this in front of a mirror with your hands resting on your ribcage so that you can easily see and feel if your ribcage expands and if your shoulders stay down. Use this easy and quick technique for alert or complete relaxation. A perfect time to do circular ribcage breathing is before you skate into a difficult element, as well as throughout your program.

Focused ribcage breathing. If you are feeling tense, nervous, angry, frustrated, or any way that usually leads to over-activation, imagine positive energy and confident, calm feelings enter your body as you inhale, while negative thoughts and tense, out-of-control feelings leave your body as you exhale. Focus on how you want to feel each time you inhale to help you achieve the relaxed feeling you desire. For example, think, *In with calm, confidence, etc.,* as you inhale, and, *Out with* *tension, stress, etc.,* while you exhale. Essentially, the idea is to think, *In with the good,* as you inhale and, *Out with the bad,* as you exhale.

A good time to use focused ribcage breathing is if you start to force your technique while trying too hard to execute an element. This problem arises when you don't trust your technique enough to allow your body to do what you have trained it to do. With no trust, your movements become forced, jerky, rushed, and/or out of control. As a result, the tension in your muscles increases as your thoughts get scattered, and the element becomes more difficult to perform than ever before. If this happens, relax with focused ribcage breathing. Focus on breathing in calmness and trust of your technique, and exhale all your doubts and tension out of your mind and body. Imagine doing the element correctly before you perform it with a quiet mind and controlled body. The objective in such a situation is to relax your mind and body, refocus your thoughts, trust your technique, and, finally, perform your best.

This technique is also helpful when you need to control your reaction to a potential stressor. In times when the only thing you can control is your reaction, sometimes it is best to respond with a breath. Breathe in how you want to feel as you face the situation with complete control, and breathe out any stress. Think of literally blowing off the stressor with each breath you release.

Cue word breathing. If you get distracted or are feeling tense, you can combine a few ribcage breaths with thinking of cue words to help you achieve your desired focus and activation level. While breathing, focus on one or more words related to your desired focus and activation level. If there is a time in your program when you usually get uptight, choreograph a ribcage breath with a cue word related to relaxed confidence immediately beforehand. For example, while setting up for one of the most difficult elements in your program, take a ribcage breath and think *Trust* to get your mind and body ready to do the element.

It is also a good idea to take a deep ribcage breath while thinking a positive cue word before you start your program to control your activation level, followed by thinking an affirmation about skating your best. For example, as you get into your starting position, take a deep ribcage breath while focusing on the word *calm, believe,* or *trust,* followed by thinking something encouraging such as *Go for it, I'm ready,* or *It's my time to shine.*

Additional uses. You can use ribcage breathing to get more out of stretches, exercises, or choreography, and it can help establish the proper timing for elements. When working breathing into your timing, keep in mind that it is best to exhale at the most demanding points of an element (inhale to prepare, exhale to execute). For example, inhale as you reach to tap for a jump and exhale as you explode into the air, or inhale as you step into a spiral and exhale as you stretch your body to its limit. Use the same timing for your breathing to get the most out of your off-ice stretches and exercises, too. Practice ribcage breathing before you think of affirmations, do imagery, or go to sleep, in order to help you relax your body and clear your mind. The longer and deeper you make your breaths, the more relaxed you will feel.

Muscular relaxation. **Active**, **differential**, and **passive** muscular relaxation techniques are all excellent to use when you want complete, deep relaxation. Use these techniques to help you go to sleep or relax after a demanding workout. You can also achieve alert relaxation with **stand-up muscular relaxation** or a quick body scan and tension release. A description of each style of muscular relaxation is explained in this section.

Active muscular relaxation. Start by focusing on ribcage breathing while you're in a comfortable position in a quiet place. Clear your mind of any thoughts, and just focus on the rhythm of your breathing. Once your breathing is deep and even, you are ready to focus on different parts of your body and relax the muscles in each area. Contract each muscle group for a count of five while you inhale, and then relax the muscles completely while you exhale for a count of six. You can think of this action as the *squeeze and release technique.* Be sure to focus on any remaining tension leaving your body each time you exhale. Repeat this sequence two times for each muscle group or until you feel all tension leave the area of your body you're focusing on.

Follow this order: Left foot, left leg, right foot, right leg, buttocks, stomach, left hand and lower arm, right hand and lower arm, upper arms and chest, shoulders and neck, and finally your face. When you finish all the muscle groups, scan (quickly focus on) your entire body from your feet to your head and squeeze and release any leftover tension that you find. Once you feel completely relaxed, say a word to yourself that you can use later as a cue word for quickly releasing tension and getting relaxed. Think *calm, relaxed, mellow,* etc. There is a script you can use for this relaxation technique at the end of this chapter.

As you get better at using this technique, you will be able to release any tension with fewer squeeze and releases. You will also be able to combine muscle groups as you improve your ability to release muscle tension. You will even be able to achieve an alert, relaxed state in only a few seconds! Simply do a quick scan of your body and release any muscle tension you notice by doing ribcage breathing with a few squeeze and releases. Think of your cue word for alert relaxation while you release any tension. This type of quick body scan is ideal to use before you skate.

Differential muscular relaxation. When you use differential muscular relaxation, each muscle group is contracted and released three times. Follow the same steps as with active muscular relaxation, but use three different levels of squeezing. During the first contraction, squeeze the muscles 100%. Only squeeze with 50% of your strength during the second contraction, and only 25% on the third contraction. Besides leading to complete relaxation, this style will also help you become aware of different levels of tension.

Passive muscular relaxation. Passive muscular relaxation is exactly the same as active muscular relaxation, except that the muscles are not contracted. Instead, focus on each muscle group as you inhale, and feel the tension release from each muscle group as you exhale. This is a bit trickier, but many athletes have such awareness of their muscles that they tend to prefer this style of muscular relaxation. Imagine any tension melting away as you exhale, and feel the warmth of your muscles as they relax. You can do a shorter version of this technique for alert relaxation. Do a quick body scan and release any muscle tension you find while you exhale and think of your cue word for alert relaxation. This type of quick body scan is ideal to use before you skate.

Stand-up muscular relaxation. This is a great technique to use before you skate or anytime you want to feel an alert state of relaxation. (If you have any spinal problems, check with your doctor or trainer before using this technique.)

Stand in a comfortable position with your knees slightly bent and take your pulse. Take several deep ribcage breaths as you clear your mind and focus on your breathing. Continue ribcage breathing while you do the following movements. Tilt your head to the left, letting your left ear drop toward your left shoulder, and repeat on the right side. Look to the left, roll your head down and around to the right, and repeat in the other direction. Stretch your arms in front of you, reach up above your head, and slowly swing your arms back and down until your arms hang loosely at your sides. Stretch your arms behind you, reach up above your head, and slowly swing your arms in front of you and down until your arms hang loosely at your sides. Roll your shoulders forward twice and backward twice, and then press your shoulder blades down and back toward each other.

Clench and release your hands. Shake out any leftover tension in your arms and hands. Do two figure eights in the air with each of your knees (one at a time, please!). Curl and release your toes. Shake away any remaining tension in your feet and legs. Think of your alert relaxation cue as you take several deep ribcage breaths. Notice that you feel calm, confident, and ready to take on whatever your day has to offer. Check your pulse to determine if it slowed down, and enjoy the rest of your day!

Perception. If you find that you are over-activated, check in with your perception of the situation. People will experience the same situation differently as a result of the many ways we can think about and interpret what is going on within and around us. Often you can relax simply by changing how you think about a situation. For example, you can think of a new element as being scary and super difficult, or you can choose to think of it as exciting and be proud of yourself for putting in the hard work to be ready to learn such an amazing element.

At an event, you can be afraid of making a bunch of mistakes, or you can be excited about having the opportunity to share what you have been practicing with everyone in the audience. You can also interpret the rush of adrenaline you feel before you perform as a bad sign that you are losing control or as a good sign that your mind and body are getting ready to perform. You can consider judges to be people who are sitting on the sidelines waiting for you to make a mistake so they can mark you down, or you can realize that they are volunteers who love skating, who choose to use their spare time to encourage skaters, and who would much rather spend their time at the rink enjoying great performances than watching ones filled with mistakes.

> *I try not to think of [competition nerves] as pressure, but as energy. I try to feel the energy [of the audience] and use it in my performance. . . . Being nervous is natural. I just try to remember I really like what I am doing.*
> **Benjamin Agosto: World Junior Dance Champion & U.S. National Dance Champion with Tanith Belbin**

It is important to realize that you create your reality by choosing how to think about or perceive a situation. Whenever you feel over-activated, do everything in your power to create a reality that makes it easy for you to be relaxed, feel confident, and enjoy yourself.

Imagery. You can use imagery for complete and alert relaxation. The idea is to use an image that allows your body and mind to relax. Experiment with using the several different relaxing imageries described in this section, and also try creating your own.

Favorite place. This is a good relaxation technique to use when you would like to momentarily remove yourself from a stressful situation but can't really leave. Using all your senses, imagine yourself at a favorite place. This place can be real or of your own creation, and you can be surrounded by friends or alone, whatever relaxes you the most. Before using this imagery, practice it and connect the relaxed feeling you get with your cue word for relaxation. With practice, just a quick flash of your favorite place in your mind while thinking the cue word will relax you in a few seconds.

Success imagery. If you are feeling nervous about a certain element or an entire program, replay in your mind the last time you were successful doing the element or program. Continue the imagery to experience the physical sensations and the feelings you had afterward. Keep in mind that if you were successful once, you can do the same again and again. This thought and imagery will help you refocus, and it will remind you that you are able to do whatever it is you are about to do. If you are learning something new or have a program that you have not skated clean yet, imagine doing the element or program well and how excited you will feel after being successful for the first time.

Color imagery. Imagine your body filled with a color that represents nervousness, tension, stress, or whatever you are feeling that is causing you to be over-activated. Then, while you inhale, imagine a color that represents calmness and confidence entering your body. Imagine the *bad* color leaving your body while you exhale, and the *good* color overtaking your body as you inhale. As your internal color changes, slowly feel your activation level adjust to how you want to feel.

Numbers. Picture a column of numbers in your mind, with 20 at the top and 0 at the bottom. Starting at the top with 20, focus on each number as you breathe in relaxation and breathe out tension. Take a ribcage breath for each number, and feel yourself sink into a more relaxed state as you work your way down from 20 to 0. You can do the same sort of imagery using a staircase or elevator instead of a column of numbers.

Floating on clouds. Imagine that you are floating on soft, fluffy clouds. As you float, feel all of your worries and tension leave your body with the gentle breeze. Feel your body relax as the sun shines on you and warms your muscles. You can even add in sounds of nature if you find it relaxing.

Distraction. Distract yourself by doing or thinking of something that does not make you feel stress – or even better, that releases stress. For example, you can read something light, talk to a friend, think of a joke, watch a movie, focus on your preparation or goals, or play a game to relax. Use this technique before you need your full attention on what you are doing.

> *I just remember how I have been training before I came to the competition. . . . When I think of that, I feel ready to go out and perform.*
>
> **Sasha Cohen: Olympian, World & U.S. National Medalist**

Meditation. Meditation involves quieting the mind and then relaxing the body. There are many varieties of meditation; one of the simplest involves focusing on your breathing and a single word, sound, or short phrase. If you think this seems to be a lot like focused and cue word ribcage breathing, you are right! Meditation is a combination of the two techniques.

Start by focusing on relaxing ribcage breaths to quiet your mind and release tension from your body. If your mind starts to wander, gently guide your focus back to your breathing. Once your mind is clear, continue focusing on your breathing while thinking or saying a calming word, sound, or phrase with each breath. *(Hint: Words or sounds starting with the letter* A *or* O *and ending with the letter* N *or* M *appear to be the most relaxing. For example, try "ohm" or "amen."*) Start meditating for a few minutes, and keep adding minutes until you can quiet your mind and relax your body for up to twenty minutes. This is a great way to relax and rejuvenate any time of the day.

Music. Pick out relaxing music and listen to it when you need to lower your activation level. The music you pick may be loud and fast or soft and mellow; it doesn't matter what type it is as long as it helps you relax when you hear it. As you listen to the music, feel all your tension melt away. You can let yourself relax as much or as little as you want. Listening to music before you skate is also a great way to block out unwanted distractions. Bring a personal music player to every event for this purpose.

Energizing

As with relaxation, there are several energizing techniques you can use to increase your activation level. Practice them all, and then decide which ones will work for you in different situations. These techniques are useful when you find yourself tired or bored during practice, not rested or a little ill before you skate, or performing more than once a day during an event.

Working through low-energy days during practice is essential to your mental toughness training, because chances are you will show up at an event sometime with low energy due to travel, illness, lack of sleep, or something else. If you stay tough during low-energy practice days and find energizing techniques that work to bring out your best, you will be able to feel confident in these techniques during an event. You will also be able to test your limits and know when to push yourself and when you need to back off a bit. However, if you never push yourself during low-energy practice days, you won't get enough practice to develop the techniques, you won't feel confident enough to handle low-energy performance days, and you will never discover just how tough you are.

Breathing. You can use ribcage breathing for energizing as well as relaxation. Follow the instructions for ribcage breathing in the relaxation section, but instead of having a slow rhythm, slightly increase your breathing rate (not too fast, because you don't want to hyperventilate!). While doing so, imagine that you are filling yourself up with energy with each inhalation and getting rid of fatigue with each exhalation. You may want to use cue words such as *energy, power,* or *strength in* as you inhale, and *fatigue, heaviness,* or *sleepiness out* as you exhale.

Imagery. Try out different imageries that make you feel strong, powerful, invincible, and able to produce your own energy. You can see yourself as a powerful animal, an energy-producing machine, a superhero, an invincible character from your favorite computer game, the battery bunny, etc. You can also imagine that you have an energy knob that you can control to activate yourself. You can use numbers by imagining a column that starts with 0 and goes up to 10 or 20 with each breath. As the numbers get larger, feel yourself increase your energy and release any fatigue. You can even imagine being on an elevator and feel your energy level rise each time you reach a higher floor.

Try using colors as you did with relaxation, except imagine colors that represent a loss of energy being replaced with powerful colors. You can also use success imagery that will pump you up. Imagine something you've already achieved or something you want to achieve. Try to feel the excitement or energy you felt (or would feel if it hasn't happened yet). If there are places in your program when you usually start to feel tired, practice flashing an energizing image in your mind and/or saying a related cue word at those points to recharge yourself.

If you are practicing and have low energy, imagine that you are about to perform at your next event. Think about how much energy and effort you would want to give to your performance, and dig deep to bring out your best for the imagined event. Give everything you have to be your best for that day. Experiment with all of these ideas or create your own to practice using imagery until you can simply flash a specific image in your mind to feel energized. Combine the imageries with cue words to make this skill even more effective.

Use the environment. You can use your environment to raise your activation level. Listen to music that pumps you up, really get into your own music if you're skating your program, feed off the crowd if you are performing, or get motivated during practice by watching skaters who are working hard.

Refocus. Instead of thinking about how tired you are, focus on what you are doing at the moment. Think about technique while you are skating. Reminding yourself of your goals and how wonderful you will feel once you accomplish them will also increase your motivation.

Cue words. You can use cue words with ribcage breaths to activate yourself. Create a list of cue words to use for this purpose to make it easier to bring them to mind when you need to use this technique.

Channel your energy. If you are feeling frustration, anger, or any potentially distracting emotion, you can channel your emotions into energy instead of letting them stress you out and then drain you. Use the initial activation you get when you have these emotions to your advantage by directing it into skating your best. For example, if you feel frustrated about a certain element, turn your frustration into intense determination to master the element.

Break it up. If you have low energy while practicing, try breaking up your training into short blocks of time (three to five minutes long). Decide to commit to giving everything you have for one block of time. Focus on the quality of your technique and be certain that you don't just go through the motions of skating. When the time is up, grade yourself on how you did. Did you hold back or did you dig deep to give your best effort? If you held back, try a different approach for another small block of time. If you were able to give your maximum effort, what did you think of to bring out your best? Try that again for the next block of time. Grade yourself again and repeat the process until the day is over.

Activation: final round

With more awareness of your optimal activation level and practice using the relaxation and energizing techniques described in this chapter, you will be able to maintain the activation level you desire both on and off the ice. Check in with yourself during your off-ice warm-up and right before you step on the ice for signs from your mind and body that you need to adjust your activation level. Be sure to remember that a little bit of extra activation before you perform is a natural, positive reaction to the situation. Interpret this as a sign that you are ready to perform.

Be sure to use these techniques away from the ice anytime you think you could feel or perform better by changing your activation level. In addition to enhancing your performance, the relaxation techniques can provide important health benefits, especially for your heart and blood pressure, every time you release unwanted stress and tension. Get in the habit of checking in with your mind and body throughout the day, even when you are not skating, to keep yourself in your optimal activation level.

Message to coaches and parents

Coaches:

Try to learn the optimal activation level for each of your students and what you can do to help every student maintain that level. Encourage your students to try out different techniques for relaxation and energizing to find what works best for them. Remind your skaters to check in with their activation level before practice and events to see if any adjustments need to be made. A good time for your students to do this is during their off-ice warm-up and right before they step on the ice.

When you notice that your students are too activated (stressed, nervous, worried, or tense) during an event, ask them to use their favorite relaxation technique. Remind them that a little bit of nerves, or extra energy, is not only normal but also a good thing they can use to their advantage. Always complete this process by asking your students to focus on their successes in training, their preparation, their goals, a few cues or instructions, or their ability to perform well.

> *You should not expect to eliminate nervousness: the competitor's job is to control it and even make it work for him or her.*
> **Carol Heiss Jenkins: Olympic Champion, Olympic, World & National Coach**

When you notice that your students have low activation levels, ask them to use their favorite energizing technique. Follow this up with a discussion about how much better they will feel at the end of the day if they apply their best effort to attain their daily goals as compared to wasting the day skating poorly due to lack of commitment and exertion. Other options for motivating your students are to create new challenges for them, discuss the students' goals for the day and the next event, or have them pretend they are skating at their next event (or that they are at an audition, someone important is watching, they are on TV, and so on). Afterward, discuss what they did in their mind to bring out their best and whether it worked. If a student has extremely low energy during a lesson, ask for his or her best effort for a small portion of the lesson (between three to five minutes). Once the time is up, discuss what the student did to give his or her best effort and whether the effort was successful.

Experiment with choreographing ribcage breathing in programs, moves in the field, dances, etc. Talk about releases and focal points for each breath. Figure out how breaths can work into the timing of elements, off-ice exercises, and stretches. Keep in mind that it is best to inhale to prepare and exhale to execute a movement. If your students are angry or frustrated, stop the possible downward spiral effect as soon as you notice the change in their demeanor. Confront them by encouraging them to take control of themselves by doing a relaxation exercise, followed by either replacing emotional thoughts with logical thoughts or channeling their burst of energy into determination. If students are discouraged and down on themselves, try to get them out of their heads with reassurance and support. Remind them of past successes to help them regain some positive energy, and ask them to focus on one or two simple cues or instructions.

Make a commitment to use the relaxation and energizing techniques yourself, too! Maintaining your optimal activation level is essential to your success as a coach, because most of your students will be sensitive to your stress and energy levels. Check in with your activation level several times a day to see if you need to make an adjustment. These techniques are well worth mastering because not only can your activation level have a negative or positive impact on your students; it can have an even greater impact on your own health.

Parents:

Make an effort to learn where your child's optimal activation level is for both practice and events. Discuss with your child what you can do to help him or her relax or energize when an adjustment is needed. However, if you have this discussion you must be able to accept the fact that sometimes the best thing to do is to give your child some space. During events, do your best to keep your child away from tense people, including friends and family. If your child has low energy before practice or a performance, and is open to your suggestions, encourage him or her to do a favorite energizing exercise, to remember his or her goals for that day, and to imagine how great it will feel to complete those goals.

Keep yourself in your optimal activation zone, as well. Use the techniques covered in this chapter to deal with the stressors and energy zappers you face on a daily basis. Ribcage breathing, imagery, and scanning your body for tension are all quick methods for relaxation and can help you stay calm. If you feel nervous at an event and have difficulty calming down, give your child extra space so that he or she doesn't have to deal with your anxiety on top of everything else (most children are easily affected by their parents' anxiety).

In general, encourage your child to learn how to effectively cope with the stress of life. Trying to take all the stress out of your child's life will result in weak coping skills and a low tolerance for stress. However, doing little to protect your child from the stress of life before your child has developed the proper coping skills can be overwhelming for the child. The key is to find a healthy compromise between creating an unrealistic, low-stress environment with minimal disappointments and a high-stress environment that will likely result in an overwhelmed child with a broken spirit. Think about the development of these coping skills like building muscles. Your child will need to face incremental challenges to become proficient in dealing with stress, just as muscles need to be worked and stressed more and more to become increasingly strong.

Mental Toughness Training Exercises

Evaluate and compare the activation level of a great performance and a poor performance

Think of a recent great performance and write your answers to the questions below in your mental toughness training journal.

1. On a scale from 1 to 10, rank your activation level before you skated and while you skated (1 is extremely relaxed and 10 is super energized).
2. What did your body feel like?
3. Did you feel like you had control of your body?
4. What was going on in your mind? What thoughts did you have while you were skating?
5. Could you control your focus? Where was your focus directed while you were skating?
6. In what ways did you feel similar to how you feel during practice? In what ways did you feel different?
7. What else do you remember about your activation level?

Now answer the same questions while you think about a recent poor performance. Compare your evaluations and describe the similarities and differences in your journal. Use this information to increase your awareness of your optimal activation level for performances. When you find it necessary to adjust your activation level, you can use your responses as a guideline for your adjustments.

Evaluate and compare the activation level of a great practice and a poor practice

Think of a recent great practice and write your answers to the following questions in your mental toughness training journal.

1. On a scale from 1 to 10, rank your activation level before you skated and while you skated (1 is extremely relaxed and 10 is super energized).

2. What did your body feel like?
3. Did you feel like you had control of your body?
4. What was going on in your mind? What thoughts did you have while you were skating?
5. Could you control your focus? Where was your focus directed while you were skating?
6. Did you have any specific goals you were working toward? Did you complete your goals?
7. What else do you remember about your activation level?

Now answer the same questions while you think about a recent poor practice. Compare your evaluations and describe the similarities and differences in your journal. Use this information to increase your awareness of your optimal activation level for practice. When you find it necessary to adjust your activation level, you can use your responses as a guideline for your adjustments.

Think about stressors and mentally tough reactions

Create a list in your mental toughness training journal of things or situations that normally cause you stress, and describe how you usually react to these stressors. Once you complete your list, think of the relaxation and energizing techniques covered in this chapter and describe how you can better control your reaction to the potential stressors.

Think about energy zappers and mentally tough reactions

Create a list in your mental toughness training journal of situations or things that normally zap your energy, and describe how you usually react to these energy zappers. Once your list is complete, describe how you can better control your reactions by using the energizing techniques covered in this chapter (or techniques of your own creation).

List cue words

Think of cue words for relaxation and energizing, and make a list for each in your mental toughness training journal. Experiment with each of the cues to discover which ones are most effective. Add to your list when you think of other cue words that work for you.

Create a Chill Mix

Create a mix of music that you can listen to when you want to relax or *chill out*. Use technology that will enable you to listen to the mix at the rink, on the road, at home, or anywhere you may need to relax. Be sure to bring the mix with you to events, and update your *Chill Mix* at least once a year.

Make a Booster Mix

Make a music mix that you can listen to when you need a boost of energy. Use technology that will enable you to listen to the mix at the rink, on the road, at home, or anywhere you may need to energize yourself. Be sure to bring the mix with you to events, and update your *Booster Mix* at least once a year. The CD *Sport & Soul: Skate for the Love* contains four high-spirited, original songs that are incredibly motivational and perfect for a skater's *Booster Mix*.

Follow an active muscular relaxation script

You can read this script and then follow it in your mind or make a recording of the script to listen to. A recording may be more effective with relaxing music in the background.

> Sit or lie down in a comfortable position. Close your eyes and focus on your breathing. Take several deep ribcage breaths as you quiet your mind, and feel your body relax deeper and deeper each time you exhale. Let any worries leave your mind while you narrow your focus to only your breathing. If your mind starts to wander, gently guide your focus back to your breathing . . .

Once you feel more relaxed and your mind is quiet, curl your left toes while you breathe in, and pause . . . Now relax your foot as you exhale . . . Curl your toes again while you inhale . . . and then feel any soreness and tension leave your foot as you exhale and relax . . .

Tighten your left leg and breathe in . . . Now relax your leg while you breathe out . . . Tighten your leg again as you inhale and pause . . . Now release and feel the leg sink down while you exhale . . .

Take a deep ribcage breath, pause, and relax as you exhale . . .

Curl your right toes and breathe in . . . now relax your foot while you breathe out . . . Curl your toes again as you inhale . . . and release the muscles and feel your foot relax as you exhale . . .

Tighten your right leg with a deep breath in . . . and release the muscles as you empty your lungs . . . Flex your leg again as you inhale, pause . . . and release as you exhale . . .

Now squeeze your bottom together as you breathe in . . . and relax as you breathe out . . . Squeeze again with a deeper breath in . . . and totally relax your muscles as you exhale . . .

Imagine you are floating on clouds . . . You're completely calm and more relaxed with every breath . . .

Now breathe in and tighten your stomach . . . and relax as you breathe out . . . Inhale again and tighten your stomach . . . and exhale as you let go of the muscles . . .

Make a fist with your left hand as you breathe in . . . and release it as you breathe out . . . Make another fist with your left hand and inhale . . . release as you empty your lungs . . .

Breathe in deeply, pause and exhale as you feel your body go deeper and deeper into relaxation . . .

Make a fist with your right hand as you breathe in . . . let the fist go limp and breathe out . . . Inhale and make another fist with your right hand . . . and release as you empty your lungs . . .

Squeeze your arms against your chest as you inhale . . . and relax as you exhale . . . Squeeze your arms against your chest with a deeper breath in . . . and release as you exhale . . .

Shrug your shoulders up to your ears and breathe in . . . drop your shoulders and let the tension melt away as you exhale . . . Shrug your shoulders up a little higher as you breathe in . . . relax and empty your lungs . . .

Clench your jaw and wrinkle your forehead as you take a deep breath in . . . and let it all go loose as you breathe out . . . Clench your jaw and wrinkle your forehead again as you breathe in deeply . . . and feel your jaw loosen and your forehead relax as you breathe out . . .

Scan your body for any leftover tense muscles . . . tighten and release those muscles while you take deep ribcage breaths . . . Slowly breathe in and out as you feel how relaxed you are . . . You are in control of your body and you feel wonderful . . . You are calm and completely relaxed . . .

While you enjoy the complete relaxation, think of your relaxation cue word and continue to breathe slowly and deeply . . . Say your cue word several times and feel yourself sinking deeper and deeper into relaxation . . .

You may now drift off to a tranquil sleep . . .

Or count from 1 to 10 as you inhale and exhale slowly ten times. Feel yourself become more alert with each number so that you are completely alert when you reach your tenth breath . . . Open your eyes with a relaxed, refreshed body and an alert mind.

Chapter 5

Use the Power of Your Imagination

> *I used visualization a lot when I was competing. . . . In fact, the night I won the Olympic Gold medal, everything happened exactly how I'd visualized it.*
> **Brian Boitano: Olympic, World & U.S. National Champion**

Negative Newt forgot his program during his first two competitions, so at the third competition he was pretty scared about forgetting it again. When he told his friend about his fears the day of the competition, his friend told him about a technique called imagery and said he should imagine skating his program a bunch of times to help him remember it. Negative Newt thought this was worth a try; but when he started to imagine his performance, he saw himself make a few mistakes. This made him even more scared, but he decided to make one more attempt at imagery. Unfortunately, the second time he imagined his performance, he saw himself making mistakes he'd never made before, and then he was really nervous. Negative Newt didn't recover his confidence before he skated, and his performance was not one he wished to remember. Needless to say, he never wanted anything to do with imagery ever again!

Positive Polly was introduced to imagery during a training camp, and she decided it sounded like a fun mental skill to learn. She followed the suggestion to start by doing imageries of things she sees and does at home before trying to use imagery to improve her skating. She had a hard time seeing clear images at first, but after a great deal of practice she was able to see sharp, detailed images. She became quite good at controlling what she imagined, as well.

Before Positive Polly learned imagery, it took her a long time to remember steps in her program, especially footwork. Much to her delight, she noticed that she mastered her program and moves a lot faster if she imagined what she learned in her lessons each night. She also felt more prepared and excited for competitions, tests, and exhibitions when she imagined being there first. She was relieved to discover that this type of mental preparation made her a lot less nervous for performances, so much so that she started to have fun at events and enjoyed skating in front of an audience more than ever.

Introduction to imagery

Most people mention imagery when asked if they know anything about sport psychology or mental skills. This mental skill is similar to a daydream, with the main differences being that you purposefully initiate imagery and you control what you imagine. Imagery is sometimes called *visualization*, *mental rehearsal*, or *mental practice*; but to avoid confusion, this mental skill is referred to as *imagery* throughout this manual.

The use of imagery can enhance your skating in many ways. For instance, imagery can aid the learning process, improve your consistency, strengthen your muscle memory, and help you prepare for upcoming events. Using imagery can increase your chances of attaining a goal by training your mind and body to believe it to be possible. Imagery can also be used for both relaxation and energizing, to overcome mental blocks, and to deal with distractions, as well as to enhance motivation and injury rehabilitation.

> *I think athletes are pretty simple machines. If you concentrate on positive images, then there's no room for any negative ones to take hold.*
> **Charlie Tickner: Olympic Medalist, World & U.S. National Champion**

Once you realize the wide variety of uses for imagery, you can bring out your Inner Champion by understanding how imagery works, practicing and improving imagery, and most important, using it often! It is common for top athletes to spend between fifteen minutes and one hour doing imageries of their sport every day!

How imagery works

Try to imagine being in a room with a blackboard, and then picture a person scratching fingernails down the blackboard. Did you feel chills or slightly squirm as you imagined it? Now think of biting into a lemon wedge. Did your mouth water, or did you scrunch your face while imagining the lemon's tartness? If you were able to get a clear image of either one of these experiences, your body probably reacted even though the blackboard and lemon did not exist. Now imagine the first time you completed a difficult element, like an axel, a complicated step sequence, your first double or triple, or a flying spin. Did your heart beat faster? Did you smile? Think of another happy time in your life. How do you feel, and what expression does that memory bring to your face? Have you ever watched a horror movie and felt extremely scared, even though you knew what you were watching wasn't real?

If you imagined all of the suggested scenarios, you might have noticed that your body doesn't know the difference between real experiences and events imagined in a realistic manner. Each time you imagine yourself doing or experiencing something, your brain sends your body messages that are similar to what would be sent if you were physically doing or experiencing the same thing. As a result, the use of this skill can improve muscle memory, increase confidence, and produce other possible benefits. For this reason, you want to make your imageries as real as possible. In other words, use all your senses to create vivid images that are full of detail. Try to see colors, hear sounds, smell scents, feel movements and sensations, and even taste things, if appropriate. Remember that the more realistic the imagery, the stronger effect it will have on your body, your confidence, your muscle memory, your learning rate, your feeling of being prepared, and, ultimately, your performance.

When you are doing skating imageries, imagine the musty scent (or whatever is appropriate for the rink) and feel the cool air hit your face as you skate. Hear your blades carve into the surface as you sail across the ice, spin, and jump. See your breath if the air is cold enough, and include all the details of the rink's decor. Hear your coach's instruction, the announcements, the music, the crowd, and any other noises that fit the situation. To further enhance your imagery, include any appropriate tastes, such as the taste of a dry mouth, sweat, or sport drinks.

Although imagery sends your body messages that are similar to reality, it can't take the place of the real thing. Imagery is most useful when used in combination with focused practices and performances. Numerous studies have compared athletes who physically practiced a skill, others who mentally practiced the same skill, and others who physically and mentally practiced the same skill. Before-and-after tests of these athletes show that the athletes who used imagery along with physically practicing the skill improved significantly faster and became more consistent than the other two groups.

Types of imagery

There are a variety of ways to experience imagery. During *external* imagery, you *see* yourself as if you are watching yourself from the audience or on a video. *Internal* imageries are experienced from your eyes' view, as if you were actually doing what you are imagining. (In other words, these two types of imagery are not unlike the different viewpoint choices available in some video games.) You can also think through imagery or just feel what you are imagining without experiencing anything visually. Although it is unclear which type of imagery is superior, a popular belief is that internal imagery using all the senses is best, because it is the most realistic. For this reason, try to develop and use fully detailed internal imagery. However, since all types have been proven to be effective, any type of imagery is beneficial – just as long as you use it. You may even find that you use a variety of types within the same imagery, which is a common practice.

How to practice imagery

It is best to relax your body of any tension and clear your mind of any thoughts before you begin imageries. By doing this, you will create a clear path between your mind's *screen* and your body. Use your favorite relaxation technique for this purpose. To practice internal imagery, start with a familiar scene. You can imagine sitting on your bed while you look at the walls and other details of your bedroom; next imagine walking around your house counting the windows, doors, and pictures on the walls. Once this type of image is clear and controlled, continue with a familiar scene that has more action, such as walking into your rink, putting on your skates, and stroking around the ice. Lastly, see yourself warming up and skating like you would on a practice session and at an event.

To practice using your senses, do imageries that include all five senses. If certain aspects of imagery are more difficult for you to gain control of than others, continue doing imageries that allow you to focus on your weaknesses. For example, if you have difficulty imagining sounds, practice imageries that include music and other sounds. If getting the feel of your imageries is difficult, practice imageries that focus on body positions and movements. The timing of your imageries is another element that you will need to master. You may find that you imagine things in slow or fast motion in the beginning. To gain control of your timing, you can play your music while imagining yourself doing your program. There are scripts of practice imageries at the end of this chapter. Use your imagination to create your own, too.

When you are ready to use imagery to enhance your skating, first practice it in a quiet, comfortable setting. As imagery becomes easier, include distractions so that your imageries will be more realistic. For example, add noises you would hear at the rink, and have people around you while you do your imageries. If you have a hard time getting a clear picture of yourself, watch a recent video of your skating and then – right away – imagine what you felt or saw. You can also practice imagery immediately after skating, while the feelings and experience are still fresh in your mind and body. If you find it difficult to imagine yourself doing a specific element, first imagine someone else doing the same element well, and slowly change the skater into you. With practice, this technique will help you to create a clear image.

Different uses of imagery: the three P's

Once you've become comfortable with imagery, you can put it to a variety of uses. Three particular helpful applications are for **practice**, **precision**, and **preparation**.

Practice. It is helpful to use imagery while you master elements. When you are learning a new element, correcting or improving a learned element, learning a move or dance, or learning or changing a program, use imagery to enhance the process. See yourself doing the element correctly from beginning to end. When working on a program, dance, or move, imagine as much as you know before and after you skate, on the way to and from the rink (if you aren't driving), before you go to sleep, and any other chance you get. The more imageries you do of new elements and sequences, the sooner you will have them committed to your memory (both mind and muscle).

After getting a clear image of the element(s) you are trying to master, use imagery on the ice. This will take a few seconds if you stand by the side of the ice, take a ribcage breath, and imagine yourself doing the element perfectly. Then physically recreate the image by skating around and completing the element. If your coach has not asked you to use imagery on the ice, talk to him or her about it before doing so. Letting your coach know that you are doing quick imageries will prevent him or her from thinking you are just standing on the side wasting time. For new programs, dances, and moves, imagine yourself completing the entire sequence before your first run-through of the day.

If you have difficulty imagining yourself doing an element you are learning, imagine someone else who can do it correctly. Then slowly replace the face with your face, and the body with your body. Try imagining the movements in slow motion, as well. Once you have a clear image, speed up the movement within each imagery until you complete the element in real time. If you have difficulty imagining yourself doing a jump or move you have *lost,* watch a video of the last time you did the jump or move to help you get the image. If you don't have a video, try to remember back to the last time you did it correctly and imagine what you did, what you thought, and how it felt. After getting a clear image of the element, just go do it. This is also an effective technique to use when you find yourself in a *slump* or experiencing a *mental block* with a particular element.

Precision. It is highly desirable to be able to perform all elements and programs consistently. Imagining yourself executing individual elements and your programs will help you reach this goal. Whenever you have a free moment, imagine yourself doing an element. You should also save at least fifteen minutes a day, preferably at night when you can quiet your mind, to do imageries of your programs, moves in the field, dances, or whatever elements you've been working on in your skating the last few practice sessions.

Preparation. Besides physically training for an event, it is important that you mentally prepare yourself. One of the most effective ways to mentally prepare is to do imageries of the event as you expect and want it to take place. Imagine the event from the beginning to the end with as much detail as possible.

Begin with arriving at the rink and finish with walking out the door happy with your performance. Include what you would physically do, how you want to feel emotionally, what you want to think and focus on, and how relaxed or energized you want to be throughout the entire event. Include details of the rink and your clothing, hear your name announced, see the judges and spectators, go through your warm-up, and so on. If you have never skated in or seen the rink before, use a generic rink layout, and then add the details of the rink once you get there. Also include expected distractions and how you want to deal with those distractions. Do this type of imagery several times in the weeks before the event, with a final imagery the night before or morning of the event. For your bigger events, you may want to use imagery to prepare yourself further in advance. Many successful Olympic athletes claim they did imageries of their events every day for several years before the actual date they competed.

You can also use a shorter version by just doing an imagery of the actual performance. Still include all the same details, and finish by getting off the ice happy with your performance. Do this shorter version several times a day in the weeks before the event, with a final short version immediately before your warm-up or between your warm-up and performance, if there is time.

> [Before I compete], my goal is to get into the zone where I can channel all my energy into my skating. I try to focus and visualize my performance, then I take that image out on to the ice.
> **Michelle Kwan: the most decorated U.S. female skater**

It is important to realize that it is a bad idea to start using this skill the day of an event. Some people don't have control over their imageries right away and often imagine themselves skating poorly before they get better at using this skill. The last thing you need before you perform is to be upset by what you imagine! The whole point is to see it, believe it, and achieve it, so get your imageries right!

Imagery for team skaters

If you skate with another person, or with a group, you can still use imagery in the same way as single skaters do. Your imageries should be just like skating with your team member(s), only you will have control of what everyone does in your imageries. When learning a new program or element, use imagery to get the feeling and timing comfortable in your mind and body. When preparing for an event, include your team member(s) in your imageries.

You can even prepare for mishaps by imagining how you would react if a certain move or element was not completed by you or your team member(s). If you don't know how you should react, discuss the options with your coach and team member(s). Of course, it is not suggested that you focus primarily on mishaps or use your imagination to come up with disasters that have never been known to happen. However, in moderation, using imagery to prepare for anything can be useful. When doing so, always follow up with at least one imagery of everything happening the way you want it to. The goal is to be prepared for the worst but still expect the best.

Imagery: final round

Be patient when learning this important skill, because while some master imagery immediately, it can take others several months to gain control of their images. Also keep in mind that *how much* you use imagery is more important than the *type* of imagery you use. It is well worth the effort it takes to gain control of your imagery, because the benefits of this skill are almost limitless. Other chapters explain how to use imagery to relax and energize, enhance injury rehabilitation, deal with distractions and pain, change self-talk, and aid goal setting.

You can also use imagery to help prepare, practice, or improve your precision with other endeavors outside skating. For example, if you are going to give a speech or have an interview coming up, imagine how you want to act, think, and speak several times before it takes place. If you need to confront someone about a controversial issue, imagine how you want the conversation to take place. Include in your imagery a variety of possible interactions with the person, all of which you are able to direct to get your desired outcome. Another great use of imagery is to plan for your future by imagining where you want to be and what you want to be doing in five, ten, or twenty years. If you can imagine it, you can also believe and achieve it!

Message to coaches and parents

Coaches:

Ask your students to imagine new elements first in slow motion and then in normal timing before their first attempt each day. If you are working on a correction or a new program, ask them to imagine themselves doing it correctly before and/or after practice every day to enhance the learning curve. If they have a hard time imagining themselves doing an element correctly, suggest that they picture someone else who does it well or watch a recording of someone else before seeing themselves repeat the element just as well. They can also try thinking through the movements before adding the visual component. Imagery is a good tool to use to deal with fear, lack of confidence, mental blocks, and slumps. The more your skaters experience success in their minds, the more they will expect it to happen.

Take the time to check in with each of your students regarding their imagery progress. It is not uncommon for some individuals to have to work at this skill for months before they gain control of the clarity or action of their images. However, with time and dedication, all of your skaters will be able to become expert imagers. You may find that some students will stay at the point of just feeling and/or thinking of what they are imagining without having any sort of visual component. This is not necessarily a problem; it is just one way of experiencing imagery. Encourage the skaters who have not made a conscious decision to experience imagery in this way to continue working on including the visual component, while assuring them that feeling and/or thinking through their imageries is still beneficial.

> *When my students practice their programs, they imagine visual markers and other details from the next competition venue. I tell them not to focus on where they are, but rather to imagine where they are going to be.*
> **John Nicks: World Pair Champion with Jennifer Nicks, Olympic, World & National Coach**

Recommend the use of imagery as part of your students' preparation for all events. In the weeks prior to an event, students can prepare on the ice by imagining that they are at the event location every time they do a performance run-through, and they can prepare off the ice by doing imageries of their performances. Imagery is also a great tool for your students to use once they're at the venue, especially between warm-up and the actual performance. However, avoid asking your students to use this skill for the first time at competition, or only at competition. It is a skill that takes time to master, and skaters often become anxious when they don't have a clear image. To make matters worse, they will be full of self-doubt if they see themselves falling and making other mistakes. The imagination can be an incredibly powerful tool once it is mastered – one that you and your students can use throughout life to attain your dreams and desires.

Parents:

Encourage your child to imagine achieving his or her daily goals on the way to the rink (only if your child isn't driving, of course!). If your child feels defeated, seems afraid, or has low energy, offer a reminder to use imagery to *see the achievable* and get back on track. Encourage your child to imagine a variety of elements and his or her programs every day before and/or after skating. Give your child time and space during events to imagine performing well before practice ice and the performance.

Use imagery to make your own dreams a reality, too. It is often true that before you can believe and achieve something, you must be able to imagine it happening. Imagine your greatest dreams as a reality, and use this powerful image to keep you motivated to do what it takes to make them come true.

Mental Toughness Training Exercises

Start with imagery practice scripts

"Bedroom" for senses and movement (5 to 10 minutes)

Sit or lie in a comfortable position, close your eyes, and focus on your breathing. Take deep ribcage breaths, and feel any tension leave your body as you exhale. Continue focusing on your breathing as you quiet your mind and put away any worries. Once your mind is quiet and your body is relaxed, imagine yourself sitting on your bed. Look around at the four walls and see what you have hanging on them. While looking around, notice what your bed feels like. Is it soft, lumpy, or hard? Is your bed made? What colors are your walls? Is your closet open or closed? If you have a stereo, is it on or off? What about a TV? What does your room smell like? Get up and walk over to a window, and open it if it is closed. Feel the breeze on your face. Is it warm or cold? (If you don't have a window, skip this part.) Is there anything on the floor? Find something that is out of place, and pick it up and put it away. What is it? What does it feel like? Take one more look around, and then slowly open your eyes.

Were you able to complete all parts of this imagery? Keep practicing it until you can. Keep notes of your progress in your mental toughness training journal.

"Rink" for senses and movement (5 minutes)

Sit or lie in a comfortable position, close your eyes, and focus on your breathing. Take deep ribcage breaths, and feel any tension leave your body as you exhale. Continue focusing on your breathing as you quiet your mind and put away any worries. Once your mind is quiet and your body is relaxed, imagine yourself walking into your rink. Are you pushing or pulling the door open? As you walk in, notice the change in temperature and the smell in the air. Go out by the ice and look around. What time is it? What is going on out on the ice? Is anyone skating? What color is the ice? Are all the lights on or is the rink dimly lit? What sounds do you hear? Is the ice clean, or does it need to be resurfaced? Are the gates open or closed? Take a final look around and open your eyes.

Were you able to answer all of the questions about the rink? Which senses are easier to use and which senses are more difficult to use? Keep notes of your ability to use your senses in your mental toughness training journal. Use this information to further develop the senses that are difficult to include in imageries. Continue to do imageries that focus on those senses until it is fairly easy to make your imageries vivid and realistic using all your senses.

"Skating" for movement and senses (15 to 30 minutes)

Relax and imagine you are at your rink. Go through your off-ice warm-up routine and put on your skates. Walk to the ice surface, step on, and stroke around. When this is easy to imagine with feeling, go through your normal warm-up sequence. As you do this, include all your senses. Smell the rink's scent, feel the cold air, see the decor and lighting, hear the sounds, feel your muscles working and the rhythm of your movement, etc. If you have difficulty imagining a certain element, think through it and go on to the next part of your warm-up. Continue through your warm-up until you have done a variety of elements.

Are you able to control your imagery? Do this imagery until it is easy to imagine the variety of elements you are able to do. If you have difficulty with imagining a certain element, watch yourself on video and close your eyes to imagine what you saw. If that does not work, imagine someone else doing it and then slowly turn that person into yourself. Keep track of your progress in your mental toughness training journal.

"Program" for movement and timing

You will need a copy of your program music for this imagery. If you skate only compulsory dances, use that music instead. The purpose of this exercise is to master the timing of your imageries and to continue enhancing your ability to control your imagined movements. Some people prefer to use a personal music player with headphones when listening to music with imageries, while others would rather hear the music from speakers. You can experiment with both to see which works best for you.

Cue your music before you relax and clear your mind. When you are ready, play your music and imagine yourself skating your program on private ice in an empty building. If you get ahead of or behind the music, try to get your movements back on time with the music. Replay your music several times in a row when you practice this element of imagery.

As you get comfortable with this imagery, place more focus on the technique and artistic quality of your skating. Try not playing your music; instead imagine the music playing in your mind while simultaneously imagining your program. Use a stopwatch and time yourself to see if you have the correct timing. Eventually add in other skaters, additional noises, people on the sides, and any other details from a practice session. As with all imageries, use your senses and add in a variety of details to make your experience as realistic as possible. Keep track of your progress in your mental toughness training journal.

Now try imageries to enhance your skating

Learning new elements or improving existing elements

Use imagery to help your body and mind understand the movement and timing of new or improved elements. Make sure you have a clear understanding from your coach of what you should be doing. Start by doing the imagery in slow motion in order to focus on the proper technique. Then do imageries of the element with the true timing over and over until you get a clear image. Continue doing this imagery until you are able to do the element consistently well on the ice. Go through the imagery before you skate, while you are on the ice before you do the element, and at night before you sleep. Remember to use video and images of other skaters if you have difficulty getting a clear picture of yourself doing the element.

New programs, dances, and tests

When learning a new program, moves test, or dance, you can use the skill of imagery to increase your learning curve. Each day you learn new sequences, go over them in your mind before you sleep that evening. Find the time to do several more imageries of what you know before you return to the ice to learn more. When you know the entire program, test, or dance, continue doing imageries each day until you are comfortable on the ice. Once the sequence of elements is committed to mind and muscle memory, use imageries to help improve your consistency on the ice and to prepare for upcoming events.

Events

Use long- and short-version imagery to mentally prepare for all events. (You should master this mental skill before using it in this manner!) In the long version, begin the imagery with your arrival at the building; or if you like, include scenes of you waking up ready to skate, feeling confident at your home or hotel before you leave for the rink, skating on any practice ice, and riding to the rink. You can imagine these scenes in a *news flash* manner, so that you just flash a quick image of each scene. The short version starts when you are announced and it is time to perform.

End both versions with feeling happy and proud of yourself and the effort you put into your performance. Incorporate as many details as possible, including your desired emotions, thoughts, energy level, and focus; the feel of your body; details of the rink; the judges and audience; the announcements; the warm-up; possible distractions and how you deal with them; and any other details that will make the imagery realistic. If you have never skated in or seen the rink before, use a generic rink layout, and then add the details of the rink once you get there.

Start doing these imageries a few weeks before an event. Do at least two long versions each week and several short versions each day. Keep in mind that the more imageries you do, the better prepared you will be when the time comes to perform. Do your final long-version imagery the night before or morning of the event. Go through your final short-version imagery immediately before your warm-up or between your warm-up and performance. The track entitled *Time to Shine* on the *Sport and Soul: Skate for the Love* audio CD was designed to lead you through the long-version imagery and has proven to be a highly effective tool for skaters.

Chapter 6

Stay Focused

There is some pressure to defend our national title, but we don't focus on it. Our coach, Lynn Benson, never mentions winning. Our focus is on giving our best performance.
**Members of the Haydenettes:
U.S. National Synchronized Champions**

Negative Nettie was constantly being told she needed to concentrate better, but no one ever told her how. She was easily distracted on the ice, at school, and even at home. Her mind always wandered off from what she was doing at the moment or raced from one thing to the next. Often she got frustrated on the ice because even when she thought of the five to ten things that would make what she was doing better, her body felt so confused that nothing worked right. Soon after the confusion, her mind became overloaded before practically shutting down and going blank. Unfortunately, it seemed easy for Negative Nettie to focus on all of the things that had gone wrong in the past and what might go wrong in the future.

Positive Pete began his competitive career with disastrous results. Although he was well prepared for his early competitions, he started to doubt his training to the point of losing his confidence as soon as he saw the other skaters in his group. He also wanted to win so badly that he seemed to think of nothing but beating the other skaters while he performed.

Despite his preparation, Positive Pete never did perform very well until he attended one helpful presentation at a training camp. At the camp he learned what he could control (himself) and what he could not (other skaters and awards placement). Ever since then, he has gone into each competition focused on himself and doing his best, with mostly marvelous results. Positive Pete still enjoys placing, and it is important to him to be competitive so that his chances of placing remain high, but he focuses only on what he can control when skating.

Control your attentional focus

How many times have you been told to concentrate harder or that you're just not concentrating? Everyone has probably been told this more than once! What did you do? You might have wrinkled your nose to make it look like you were concentrating more, so that you wouldn't be reprimanded again. Chances are this didn't help, because you were concentrating on concentrating instead of on what you were doing.

How many times have you been told *how* to concentrate? For most people, the answer is never. Concentration, or attentional focus control, is a mental skill that needs to be learned, practiced, and mastered just like any other mental or physical skill. This important mental skill involves choosing where to focus your attention, understanding how to deal with distractions in order to keep the appropriate focus, being able to have the appropriate focus for the required time, and knowing how to shift from one focus to another when necessary. No matter what you are doing, there are four aspects of attentional focus that should never change. Your attentional focus should be positive, in the present, centered on things that are under your control, and as simple as possible.

Positive. Make a habit of looking for the positives in every situation, and purposely focus on those points. Always focus on what you want to *do* instead of what you want to avoid, similarly to how you approach goals and self-talk. For example, if you need to focus on keeping your right side up on a take-off, focus on keeping it *up* instead of focusing on not dropping it down.

Present. Keep your focus *in the here and now,* because you have no control over the past or what happens in the distant future. While you're skating, stay focused on the element you are doing, or, if you just finished an element, on what you are preparing to do next. In other words, take one element at a time. You should not let your focus jump too far ahead of what you are doing or get stuck on something that already happened.

If you allow your focus to stay on a mistake, you are likely to get frustrated, make another mistake, lose more of your focus, get more frustrated, make additional mistakes, and so on. This can happen because mistakes are more likely when you are tense from reacting to frustration and when you are not focused on what you are doing. Even doing something fantastic can cause problems if you lose your focus on what you are doing by celebrating before your performance is over. Focusing too far into the future can be equally devastating. Mistakes are likely when this happens because the focus is not on what is going on at the time, and focusing on the future often creates mental anxiety along with physical tension.

When top skaters are interviewed after a poor performance, they often mention something about their attentional focus. They might describe how they were not able to get their mind off the mistakes they made early in the program or how they thought too much about the most difficult element instead of taking one element at a time. They might also explain how they thought they had it made after completing the most difficult element, which led them to lose their focus and miss the easier elements.

Control. As is the case with goals and self-talk, you want to focus on things that are under your control. Focus on whatever *you can do* to achieve what you are striving for at any given moment. Your technique, effort, thoughts, emotions, and activation level are some things that you can control. Things that are not under your control include the past, the future, outcomes of events, competitors, parents, coaches, the audience, poor judging, a grueling event schedule, the media, jetlag, altitude, obnoxious people, and unforeseen changes at an event. Many skaters have been disappointed because they were so focused on their possible placement, what their competitors were doing, or wanting to impress someone that they forgot to focus on what they were doing.

> *[I now try] to look at my skating instead of looking at . . . what other people are doing. I've learned to focus on just enjoying myself out there [and to take] one step at a time.*
> **Sasha Cohen: Olympian, World & U.S. National Medalist**

Be certain you don't give your competitors any power over your performance. As long as your competitors don't sneak out on the ice and get in your way while you perform (I have never heard of this happening), they have nothing to do with how well you can skate – unless you focus on them instead of yourself. Making comparisons, assuming they are better or more prepared than you, and focusing on beating others instead of doing your best gives your competitors power over your performance that they don't really have. To avoid this mistake, think of skating *with* the other skaters, and compete only against yourself by challenging yourself to skate your personal best.

Simple. The fewer things you focus on at one time, the better you will skate. When learning a new skill, or improving one, select one or two things to focus on at once. Try to focus on technical cues and/or feelings and sensations in your muscles. Before attempting the skill, think of the desired focus and imagine yourself doing the skill correctly, and then physically repeat what you saw automatically. Once you do the skill correctly, try to re-create the same focus and feeling. When doing a learned skill, focus on simple technical cues or re-create the correct feeling as if on autopilot. In other words, let your body do what you already trained it to do.

Make focusing easier

Two primary factors that can interfere with focus are **stress** and **fatigue**, which can be mental, physical, or both! By staying aware of these factors and dealing with them immediately, you can make it easier to focus like a champion.

Stress. Mental and physical stress interfere with your ability to focus by disturbing the messages your brain and body send to each other. If you notice any stress in the form of worries and/or muscular tension, do a relaxation technique to release the stress. Make it a habit to clear your mind of any extra thoughts prior to skating, especially before having a lesson or performing. This is a simple, yet highly effective way to make focusing easier. Think of it as *checking your worries at the door* so that your mind is ready to work when you step on the ice.

Fatigue. Mental and physical fatigue also interfere with your ability to focus. If you feel physically tired, but must go on, avoid focusing on your fatigue by using an energizing technique to help you refocus on the task. If you're mentally tired, you may find yourself easily distracted and more likely to make mistakes because of an inappropriate focus. This will make you waste physical energy as well, because with the wrong focus it takes more effort to complete a task. If you are mentally fatigued, you must refocus by releasing any unnecessary thoughts or distractions. Follow up with an energizing technique and refocus on the task.

Identify distractions

A distraction can be anything that is not directly related to your task at hand (the process of skating and relevant cues). Things that are not under your control are also distractions, even if they are related to your task. Noise, spectators, negative thoughts, thoughts unrelated to skating, the announcement of your competitors' marks, frustrations, past events, the outcome of events, judges, the expectations of others, the media, and competitors can all be distractions.

> *When we are competing our minds aren't focused on what's going on around us. We are focused on the skating program that we have to perform.*
> **Naomi Lang and Peter Tchernyshev: Olympians & U.S. National Dance Champions**

Deal with distractions

There is an unlimited number of ways to deal with distractions. Several distraction control techniques are described in this section. After reading the descriptions, imagine yourself being distracted while skating, and try out the various techniques. This will allow you to discover which ones work best for different types of distractions. Once you are able to successfully deal with distractions in your imageries, try using the techniques on the ice. The last step in learning these techniques is to be able to use them to clear your mind and get focused before skating, and to successfully refocus when faced with distractions, particularly when you're under pressure.

The Four R's. The Four R's are *recognize, relax, release,* and *refocus.* First you must *recognize* that you are distracted and what the cause is. Then *relax* your mind and body by doing a ribcage breath, and *release* the distraction from your focus while you exhale. Finally, *refocus* on the task by using a cue word or image to help redirect your focus. The cue word or image should relate to the technique or feeling required for the task.

Channel Clicking. Think of your mind and focus as a TV with different screens for different focuses. When you find that you have been distracted and are on the wrong *channel,* think of changing the channel back to the one you want. Imagine you have a remote control or *channel clicker* to help you do this. You may find that taking a ribcage breath between changing channels will help you regain your focus. Think of the desired channel as **THE *(your name)* CHANNEL.** This channel will focus only on you (and some select others when you are receiving instructions or if you are part of a team).

Hot Air Balloon. Imagine a big, beautiful hot air balloon tied down to the ground. See the balloon in detail with the colors and patterns that you like. Once you have a clear picture, imagine putting whatever is distracting you into the balloon's basket. If the distraction is not a physical thing, picture something that symbolizes it. Lastly, cut the ties holding the balloon's basket to the ground. See the balloon with your distractions in the attached basket floating away until it disappears. Finish by returning your focus to your present task.

File It. Imagine you have a file cabinet somewhere in your mind or in an imaginary office/room. Use this cabinet to file away distractions that you will need to deal with *after* you skate. For example, you may have a deadline coming up, be in the middle of an argument that started before you skated, or have something stressful going on in your life that is distracting your focus while you skate. Make a file for these things, and file the distractions away and out of your mind so you can focus only on what you are doing at the time. Pull the file and deal with the distraction when you have finished skating. If the distraction is something that you don't have to deal with later, get rid of it completely by filing it in the lower, bottomless drawer where it will be sucked away and out of your mind for good.

Park It. Imagine sending, tossing, or putting the distraction away somewhere, such as up in a tree, inside a locker, under a bench, away on a train, in a jar, over the rink's railing, etc. Think of it as *parking* the distraction in whatever you decide to use. If the distraction is something you should not ignore forever, you can bring it back *after* you skate. Some people like to write descriptions of distractions on paper and keep them in a real jar or box.

Colors. If a feeling is distracting you, such as frustration, anger, or nervousness, imagine the feeling as a color that has filled your body. Then, while doing ribcage breaths and thinking *In with the good* as you breathe in and *Out with the bad* as you breathe out, imagine the unwanted color being overtaken by a color that represents calmness and confidence. Refocus on what you are doing once the calm, confident color and feelings have taken over your body.

Shrink It. Picture the distraction as something huge and unmanageable. Then imagine it shrinking down to the size of a pebble and throw it away, or make it disappear completely. Follow this with a ribcage breath and refocus on the task. For example, if you have a fear of a jump, imagine a huge *jump monster*. Then picture the ugly jump monster melting into a puddle that disappears. Take a ribcage breath, tell yourself you are capable of doing the jump, imagine yourself doing the jump, refocus on the proper technique, and go do it!

Flick It. If a person is the distraction, you can imagine the person in miniature size standing on your shoulder, then flick the person off your shoulder with your fingers. Again, you want to finish by returning your focus to the task you are doing. This technique is perfect for irritating competitors.

Turn It Down. Use this if the distraction is a noise, coming either from within your mind in the form of thoughts or from the environment. Think of having a volume control for the distraction and turn it down until you can't hear it. Better yet, turn it off.

Zoom Lens. Think of your focus as a camera lens and zoom in or out so you can get your focus off the distraction and on to what you are doing.

Flush It. Imagine flushing the distraction down a toilet. You can put it in a trash compactor, garbage disposal, or shredder, as well.

Delete It. Imagine your mind has a delete button that you can use to delete distractions from your focus. You can also send distractions to the recycle or trash bin.

Zap It. If you like to play computer games that involve *zapping* items from the screen, you'll have fun with this technique. Imagine that your focus is like a computer screen and *zap* distractions away as you would in your favorite game.

Deal with It. If the distraction is something that you have control over, deal with it by getting rid of it or changing it. If you can't control it and it is something that you have to deal with, do so to the best of your ability. For example, maybe the condition of the ice is really bad. That is something you can't change, and you can't simply ignore it, so figure out the best way to deal with it (get into your knees and ankles more, stay away from a really rough or thin patch of ice as much as possible, etc.). Ask your coach for suggestions if you can't figure out how to deal with a certain situation. If you have a hard schedule, don't just ignore it. Deal with it by making sure you get as much rest as possible and the proper nutrition, as well as using relaxation and energizing techniques.

Intensify. It is difficult to intensely focus on more than one thing at a time, especially opposing or unrelated items. Block out a distraction by focusing on what you want with extreme intensity.

Imagine. If you are distracted by doubts, imagine being successful. Keep that image in your mind until it is time to actually perform what you previously doubted. It is difficult to imagine two scenes at once, so choose to focus on a positive one!

Blow It Off. Use focused ribcage breathing to blow off a distraction. Blow off the distraction as you breathe out. Breathe in how you want to feel as you refocus.

Protective Shield. Imagine that there is a protective shield around you, and you are able to control what enters through the shield and what bounces off it. Set the controls so that all distractions bounce off the shield.

Recover from mistakes

Everyone makes mistakes, but not everyone recovers from them as quickly as they can. There is no rule in this sport stating that skaters must get frustrated, angry, or lose their confidence if they make a mistake or something doesn't go their way. You may get a deduction, but you don't have to let one mistake ruin your performance. You also don't have to doubt yourself the next time you do that element.

When you make a mistake while performing or conducting a run-through of a performance, the best thing you can do is to leave the mistake in the past where it belongs. Change your focus to the next element as quickly as possible. Channel clicking is a technique that works well in this type of situation. Once you finish the performance or run-through, you can look back and evaluate what you did and didn't do. Learn the lessons from the experience, and use that information to make yourself a better skater.

> You just have to refocus [after a mistake] and save the rest of the performance because . . . the whole dance can go to pieces.
> **Jerod Swallow: Olympian & U.S. National Dance Champion with Elizabeth Punsalan**

If you make a mistake while practicing an element, you should take time to evaluate the mistake immediately. Without letting emotions get in the way, determine what went wrong, and make the correction. This evaluation process is especially important after a hard fall to combat any fear of attempting the element again. By understanding what went wrong, you can feel confident that a correctable mistake caused the fall, instead of feeling that the element is too difficult and scary to try again. If you don't know what is causing a mistake and you keep repeating it, ask your coach for help during your next lesson.

Increase your attentional focus endurance

The amount of time you need to be able to control your attentional focus depends on what you are doing. A program can last several minutes and requires an intense focus the entire time. A moves in the field test can take up to fifteen minutes, with short breaks between moves when you can relax your focus. A practice session lasts much longer and may have short periods to relax your focus as well. You can increase the length of time you are able to control your focus simply by practicing to focus for a specific amount of time. Follow the directions for the focus endurance exercises at the end of this chapter to improve this aspect of attentional focus.

Change your type of focus

Your focus can be *wide* or *narrow*, like a zoom lens on a camera. At the same time, your focus can be *internal* (things within you, such as thoughts and body positions) or *external* (everything going on around you). Your focus can also be *motivational*, *instructive*, or more on *autopilot*.

Once you know what to focus on throughout a performance or practice session, you will need to be able to change your focus at the right time. While skating, an internal focus that is either wide or narrow is usually most appropriate; the proper focus depends on what kind of thoughts or feelings will help with what you are doing. Your internal focus should be instructive when you are learning something or motivational when you need a burst of mental or physical energy. For example, if you need to think of a specific technical cue, such as lifting your left hip during a move, then your focus needs to be not only narrow and internal, but also instructive. On the other hand, if you need to feel powerful and full of energy, your focus should be motivational, as well as wide and internal.

You can use an autopilot focus when you've already mastered something and just need to trust your technique to let your body do what it has already been trained to do. This sort of focus allows you to quiet your mind and feel your way through an element or program as opposed to thinking your way through. Lastly, a wide or narrow, external focus is needed to relate to audiences, to be aware of your patterns on the ice, and to be aware of other skaters on the ice during practice.

Both on and off the ice, you can practice changing your focus by purposely switching from one type of focus to another and then back again. Be sure to know what type of focus you need throughout your program, and practice making the necessary changes of focus. If, after reading this section, you are unsure of what you should focus on during your program, review the information at the beginning of this chapter. If you are still unsure, discuss it with your coach.

Attentional focus for team skaters

In addition to following the advice covered in this chapter, it is important for team skaters to stay focused on the role they play on their team. Before each season, figure out what your role is and what you can bring to the team. What is under your control that you can focus on to bring the most possible to the team? For example, being an alternate can be frustrating, but an alternate can play an invaluable role on a team. If you are an alternate, figure out all the ways you can contribute to the success of the team. To avoid frustration, focus on your team role, why you skate, and what you can learn throughout the season. Maybe you are the calming factor of your partnership, or maybe you are the greatest source of optimism and high energy. Whatever your strengths and contributions may be, they are most effective when you are aware of them.

How a team deals with mistakes is crucial to their success. If a team member makes a mistake during practice or a performance, avoid placing blame on that person. It is best if skaters and coaches embrace the idea that it takes a team effort to succeed just as much as it does to recover from mistakes. Playing the blame game will only tear a team apart, but sticking together through good times and bad will make the team stronger. If a mistake is made, it is best to focus on how to fix the problem and move on.

> *We don't get mad at each other when the other messes up. We are a team and we stick together. Making a mistake at competition makes us want to work hard in practice to perfect that particular element.*
> **Tiffany Scott: U.S. National Pair Champion with Philip Dulebohn**

Attentional focus: final round

Have fun when you skate, love what you do, be passionate, and enjoy each moment as much as possible to make it easier to focus on what is under your control. Approaching skating and other endeavors in this way will help you to stay relaxed and to expect the best from yourself. Every moment in which you focus on something out of your control, especially if it is a potential stressor, robs you of the positive energy and effort you could put toward doing your best.

Use your off-ice warm-up to prepare both your mind and your body to skate. Focus on your muscles getting warm as you narrow your focus and direct your energy toward what you are doing each moment. Before you step on the ice, clear your mind of everything except the purpose for the day. Check in with yourself throughout practice and events to see if you are focusing on what is most effective for your goals. Figure out if your focus is making the most of each moment in time. Instead of focusing on what you can't do, what you can't control, or what isn't working, focus on what you can do, what you can control, and what is working.

Keep in mind that you can't control lots of things, but you can control yourself and your reactions. Be creative in how you deal with distractions, and keep training your attentional focus endurance. Be confident that you can handle any situation – trust yourself, trust your training, and just do your best! As always, apply these techniques to your activities outside the ice arena to get the most you can out of your life!

Message to coaches and parents

Coaches:

Encourage your students to stay focused on things that are under their control, such as their technique, effort, focus, attitude, and activation level. If they start to get distracted by things that are out of their control (judges, other skaters, results, past events, the distant future, opinions, the media, and so on), ask them to use their favorite distraction control technique to change their focus back to themselves, the present, and the positive.

Avoid making comparisons between your students and other skaters, even if a comparison makes your students look better. Instead, focus on each student's strengths and weaknesses as they relate to the student's individual improvement and what is expected at his or her level of skating. An exception to this philosophy will arise each year when the Inner Champion Circle meets to create goals for the competitive season. At that point, it will be necessary to evaluate other skaters or teams at the same level to gain an understanding of what will be required to be competitive. However, once the level of competition has been established, the focus should return to the strengths and improvement of the skater or team.

> *At the beginning of the season, we will compare our strengths and weaknesses to our major competitors. Midway into the season, the total focus is on our team and how good we can make it.*
> **Lynn Benson: World & National Coach, Coach of the most successful U.S. Synchronized Team, the Haydenettes**

You can support your students in their effort to stay aware of their focus by checking in with them during lessons. Find out what they are focusing on when they skate great and when they skate poorly. By working together with your students, you can help them discover what type of focus is working and what should be changed. Use this information to remind them of the best focus before they start something or, when necessary, to help them get back on track. Emphasize what your students and teams have control over during practice and events, and focus on the process more than the outcome of both elements and events.

When your students are having a hard time making a correction, ask them to describe their focus throughout the element. If they answer, *I don't know,* chances are that their focus isn't in the right place! Another way to check in with your students' focusing skills is to ask them to summarize each lesson. It will be helpful for both your effectiveness as a coach and the development of your students' focusing skills if you compare what you tried to teach with what your students think they learned during their lessons. It is far too common for coaches to think they discovered an amazing breakthrough during a lesson, when the student was not aware that any change or correction was made!

Be aware of different learning styles when deciding where and how a skater should focus. Skaters will have difficulty learning if they are given information in a manner not suitable to their learning style. Some skaters learn best by seeing things done properly (visual), some skaters learn best by hearing technical instructions (auditory), some skaters learn best by feeling how to do the correct positions and timing (kinesthetic), and most learn best with a combination of two or three styles. Develop various teaching techniques that suit all three styles, and alter your type of instruction to suit your students' needs. For example, if you notice that a student is a predominantly visual learner, show the position and timing you desire, followed by having someone demonstrate the element properly while you point out various aspects of the element. If no one can demonstrate the proper technique, use a visual recording instead.

When you are teaching an element or making a correction, it is necessary to prioritize the behaviors you desire from your students. The human brain can focus on only one to three related things at once (three is pushing it), so pick one or two key aspects of each stage of an element to focus on at a time. Keep your instruction and corrections as simple as possible, relate new elements to previously learned behaviors as often as you can, acknowledge effort and small improvements, and focus on what you want your students to do instead of what you want them to avoid. Encourage patience, as well.

> *At the end of a lesson do a quick review of what you covered and then ask your pupil to give it back to you. . . . You may be surprised at how little comes back. But, if you put it in your lesson system they will improve faster and listen better.*
> **Peter Dunfield: Olympic, World & National Coach**

Employ the concept of cue words and phrases during lessons by summarizing your instruction with a cue word or phrase before a skater tries an element or makes a correction. Suggest to your students that they should focus on these cue words and phrases outside their lessons as well as record them in their journals. When you're helping a student create or correct a habit, expect the process to take approximately twenty-one days before it becomes a part of his or her muscle memory.

Talk to your students and teams about how you would like them to deal with mistakes. When should mistakes be analyzed? Is this different in practice and during a performance? When should mistakes be left behind for good? It is also helpful to discuss what you want your students to focus on while they perform.

If you coach a team, discuss the desired focus of their performances with the entire team to make certain everyone is on the same page. Also, ask all members to consider what they can bring to the team and the role they see themselves playing. To make sure that all team members are aware of everything they can contribute to the team's success, hold a team meeting to discuss this topic. To keep a positive team atmosphere, remind the team throughout the season to keep focused on their roles and contributions.

Create a plan of action for events, try to stick to the same routine as much as possible, and be prepared to deal with distractions and unexpected situations in a calm, levelheaded manner. Be a role model by staying focused on what you can control, and avoid gossiping about or focusing on other skaters, parents, coaches, and judges. Immediately before and during events, focus on your students' strengths. It is too late to do anything about weaknesses at that point, so wait until after the event to return your attention to areas needing improvement!

If you don't like the outcome of an event or a day, figure out how the process can be improved in the future. Part of your evaluation should include taking a look at the effect you have on your students and teams. Do they perceive you as a distraction, or do you help them focus? If you are uncertain, discuss your effectiveness with your students and teams.

Parents:

Be the best role model you can be by keeping your focus simple, on the present moment, on the positives, and on what you can control; encourage your child to do the same. Stay away from drawing comparisons with other skaters, even if it makes your child look better. If your child makes comparisons, encourage a focus on his or her own abilities instead. This approach will benefit your child's self-worth, strengthen intrinsic motivation, and encourage the pursuit of personal challenges that are completely under your child's control.

Avoid interrupting your child during practice time (hand motions included!) to allow your child to train physically (body awareness) and mentally (focusing skills) without unnecessary distractions. One of the primary objectives of training time should be for the skater to train like he or she wants to perform, so that performing is as similar as possible to what is done each day. Instruction, feedback, encouragement, nagging, and other forms of contact from parents are not allowed during events while a child is skating, so don't allow such contact to happen while your child is training (even if your child initiates it).

Leave the coaching to the coaches off the ice, too. It bears repeating that getting technical advice from you can lead to confusion for your child, diminish the effectiveness of your role as your child's biggest fan, and undermine your child's respect for the coaches' feedback when your recommendations are not in agreement with the coaches'. If you do have a technical concern about your child's skating, it is best to discuss the issue with the primary coach instead of with your child.

During events, many skaters are distracted by how much their family has spent and sacrificed to get them to where they are. Such a distraction can be an unnecessary, added source of pressure and can easily ruin a performance. This is a common problem for skaters with parents who try to guilt their children into performing well by constantly pointing out the amount of money that has been spent and all the sacrifices that have been made for skating. You can avoid this predicament by holding your child accountable only for the responsibilities of being a committed athlete and by refraining from making your child feel responsible for the financial decisions you've made as an adult leader of the family.

> *Kristi was always aware that skating cost money. . . . But we never discussed exact amounts with her or made money an issue for her to be concerned about, because money is not the child's concern, it's the parents'.*
> **Carole Yamaguchi: Mother of Olympic, World & U.S. National Champion Kristi Yamaguchi**

Strong reactions (positive or negative) once competition groups are posted are not recommended. Remind yourself and your child that successful competitors skate with, and not against, the others in their group as they compete against their own personal best. Allow your child time and space at events to get focused on the task at hand. Avoid last-minute instructions before your child takes the ice during events, which can be confusing and stressful. Instead, a simple *Have fun, I am proud of you,* or *Enjoy your performance* is best. Emphasize the importance of the process more than the outcome of each event by evaluating and celebrating the performance and not just the result. If you don't like a result, decide whether you can do anything different to improve the process.

Mental Toughness Training Exercises

Practice focused ribcage breathing

Take twenty ribcage breaths while counting backward from twenty to one. Stay focused on your breaths and on your body relaxing. Let any thoughts or distractions that come into your mind pass through your focus as you attend only to your breaths and your body relaxing. See how many numbers you can get through without being distracted. If you do lose your focus, momentarily tune in to what is distracting you, and then change your focus back to your breathing and counting. Start with a higher number as your focusing skills improve. Keep track of your progress in your mental toughness training journal.

Find techniques for dealing with distractions

In your mental toughness training journal, make a list of what usually distracts you during practice. If you can't think of many distractions now, practice for a week, and pay attention to when and why you lose your focus. Once you have created a list, think about which techniques will work to restore your focus for each distraction. (Review the various distraction control techniques covered in this chapter and even create some of your own.) Use imagery to try different techniques for each distraction. Once you can successfully deal with distractions in your imageries, use the same techniques on the ice. Complete this exercise by noting in your list which techniques work best for each type of distraction.

Prepare for distractions during events

To better prepare yourself for dealing with distractions during events, complete the following list before every event:

1. Describe in your mental toughness training journal your desired focus for each phase of the event.
2. Write a list of the possible distractions.

3. Decide how you want to deal with each of the distractions, including ways to deal with surprise distractions.
4. Use imagery to practice dealing with the distractions. Imagine being at the event, and purposely change your focus to the distractions so you can practice refocusing. However, also do imageries in which you keep the desired focus throughout the event.
5. Skate a mock event complete with expected distractions to practice your focus and distraction techniques. Ask parents and other skaters to act as the judges and audience, and ask other skaters to act as your competitors. If possible, have someone announce you and anyone else participating in the mock event.

Build your attentional focus endurance

Take notes in your mental toughness training journal after trying the following exercises. If your mind wanders while doing the exercises, gently guide your thoughts back to the desired focus. Write down what you focused on, how long you stayed focused, whether you were distracted, and if so, what distracted you and what you did about it. Notice whether you get distracted by the same types of things and what distraction control techniques work best for you.

1. Focus on a skate, a medal, or another skating item while keeping your mind free from any thoughts unrelated to the item.
2. Stand on one foot, hold a landing position, or do a spiral on the ground while keeping your entire focus on how your body feels.
3. Do the above exercise with your eyes closed, to train your *proprioception* – the awareness of your body in space – at the same time.
4. Focus on a single thought.
5. Stare into a fireplace or at a lit candle and keep an intense focus on the flame. Notice the shape, movement, and color of the flame.
6. Keep your mind clear of any thoughts.
7. Play your music and think through your program.

Learn to change focus on demand

Try these exercises to improve your ability to change your type of focus and the subject of your focus. Record your progress in your mental toughness training journal.

1. Sit in a room and focus on different sounds for five seconds each. You may hear humming from lights and appliances, creaks from the building, the ticking of a clock, noise from other people or animals in the room, and noise from outside the room. Are you making any noise? Can you hear your heartbeat, your breathing, your thoughts, or noise from sniffing or swallowing? Change your focus from loud to soft noises and from internal noises (your body and mind) to external noises (outside your body). Work up to being able to change your focus after only one second with an intense focus on each noise.
2. Sit in a room and focus on different items in the room for five seconds each. Look at items as a whole, as well as at just certain parts of each item. For example, look at a section of a window and then look out the window, or look at a picture hanging on a wall and then look at a small portion of the picture or frame. Change your focus between large and small areas as quickly as you can until you are able to achieve an intense focus on a different item every second.
3. Sit in a room and focus on how your body feels. Focus on different areas for five seconds at a time, making sure that you include both large and small areas. For example, focus on your left big toe, your lips, your right hand, your throat, your left calf, your back, your right knee, the temperature of the air touching an area of your skin, and then your stomach. Change your focus as quickly as you can until you can switch from one area to another every second.
4. Combine the first three exercises and focus on sounds, sights, and feelings that are within you and outside you. Change your focus as quickly as you can.
5. Imagine you are skating and practice changing your focus. For example, as you skate into an element, you need to have a wide, external focus to find a clear space. Next, you may need to switch to a wide or narrow internal focus to

remind yourself of a correction, and then you need to switch to a more narrow external focus as you get closer to your chosen space. Finally, you may need a different wide or narrow internal focus as you execute the beginning, middle, and end of the element. Imagine all aspects of your skating.
6. Play your music and practice changing your focus from wide to narrow and internal to external to perform the best program possible. Be sure to include interpreting the music, breathing, technical cues, activation cues, relating to the judges and audience, and working with your partner or teammates if applicable.

Identify attentional focus control strengths and weaknesses

Answer the following questions to discover your attentional focus control strengths and weaknesses. Each question relates to one aspect of your attentional focus control and is followed by advice on how to make improvements in that area, if needed. Write your answers in your mental toughness training journal and describe what action you will take if you find any weaknesses. After several weeks, go over the questions and advice again to see if you have made improvements. Continue working until you show strength in all areas.

Q. Do you make mistakes because you get bored and distracted? Do you make mistakes because you lose interest in what you are doing and your mind starts to wander to other things?
A. If you answered yes, improve your motivation by setting goals that allow you to practice with a purpose.

Q. Do you make mistakes because you get angry or frustrated and lose focus? Is it hard to shift your focus back to what you are doing when you become angry or frustrated, because you can't seem to *let go* of your feelings?
A. If you answered yes, pick a distraction control technique to change your focus from your emotions or the past and refocus on what you are doing.

Q. Do you make mistakes because you rush and don't set moves up properly?
A. If you answered yes, use a relaxation technique to lower your activation level and refocus on the proper set-up and timing before doing skills.

Q. Do you make mistakes because you don't know what to focus on (because it seems you have too many things to choose from)?
A. If you answered yes, change to a more narrow focus. Decide on one or two related things to focus on before doing elements.

Q. Do you make mistakes because you worry about skating badly and/or have negative thoughts? Is it hard to shift your focus back to what you are doing when you start to worry about making mistakes or have negative thoughts?
A. If you answered yes, use your self-talk control or distraction control techniques to stop the negative thoughts and worries. Then refocus on how to complete the skill successfully.

Q. Is it difficult to quickly figure out the patterns of other skaters while skating a freestyle session? Is it hard to anticipate what most of the skaters are about to do when you watch a freestyle?
A. If you answered yes, further develop your broad, external focus.

Q. Do you get confused trying to watch activities where there are many things happening at the same time, like a group number in an ice show?
A. If you answered yes, further develop switching from a broad, external focus to a narrow, external focus, and back to a broad, external focus.

Q. Is it difficult to bring together ideas from a number of different sources, such as creating footwork from several moves in the field steps?
A. If you answered yes, further develop switching from a broad, internal focus to a narrow, internal focus.

Q. Is it difficult to start with a little information and come up with a large number of ideas, such as choreography for a program after knowing the music?
A. If you answered yes, further develop switching from a narrow, internal focus to a broad, internal focus.

Q. When people talk to you, are you distracted by your own thoughts and ideas? Is it difficult to keep your thoughts from interfering with something you are watching or listening to?
A. If you answered yes, use a distraction control technique to quiet internal distractions when you should have a narrow, external focus.

Q. Do you have so many things on your mind that you become confused or forgetful?
A. If you answered yes, use a distraction control technique to quiet your mind and narrow your internal focus.

Q. Is it difficult to keep sights and sounds from interfering with your thoughts?
A. If you answered yes, use a distraction control technique to deal with external distractions when you should have a narrow, internal focus.

Q. Do you have difficulty clearing your mind of everything but a single thought or idea?
A. If you answered yes, use distraction control techniques to quiet your mind when you should maintain a narrow, internal focus.

Chapter 7

Take Action to Enhance Healing

> *I laughed a lot. I did whatever I could to be active, get outside, relax, and stay in touch with friends and family. The doctors said the more I participate and the more confident and positive I am, the more likely I'll come through with positive effects.*
> **Scott Hamilton: Olympic, World & U.S. National Champion, describing how he successfully conquered cancer**

Unfortunately, many skaters sustain at least one injury at some point during their skating career that requires them to alter their training schedule and intensity. The good news is that people faced with injuries – and illnesses – have discovered that their mind-body connection can play a major role in the healing process. Of course, the best solution to the problem of injuries is to prevent them in the first place. You can avoid injuries by using proper technique and following a sensible training regimen based on the *periodization method. Periodization* makes training more safe and effective by varying the intensity and type of your on- and off-ice training throughout the skating season. This increasingly popular training method is designed to prevent burnout and injuries, as well as to promote peaking for performances. To further safeguard the health of your body, be sure to warm up and cool down before and after every training session, avoid overtraining individual elements, listen to your body, maintain equipment appropriate to your skating level, and eat and sleep well.

When a skater is injured, getting back to a normal training schedule in good health as soon as possible is usually the primary objective. Instead of ignoring the mental component of physical injuries and their treatments, use your mind-body connection to enhance the healing of any injury you experience. Just as the mental aspects of your athletic performance are important, your perception, thoughts, emotions, focus, imagination, and activation level can help, hinder, or have a neutral effect on your injury rehabilitation. This is not to say that the use of mental skills will magically heal you. However, when used in combination with physical treatments, they can help speed up the healing process.

This chapter provides detailed explanations on how to use mental skills to enhance injury rehabilitation. These suggestions are followed by additional information on techniques that can help you regain top form once you are able to resume intensive training. Be sure to take responsibility for all that you can in working toward a successful recovery by using the mind-body connection to your benefit.

Goals

Use goals as you would for your skating. Setting, striving for, and achieving goals that focus on your healing will enhance your motivation and get your focus on your improvement. Keep the following points in mind.

- Set SMART and Positive goals for every treatment, physical therapy session, and so on.
- Your goals should focus on specific performance factors that can improve, such as flexibility, strength, and movement.
- Ask your doctor, physical therapist, or the professional handling your treatment to help you set appropriate goals for your healing rate.
- Write the goals in your mental toughness training journal, and keep track of your progress.

Self-talk

There are several aspects of your self-talk that are important for your healing. Follow each outlined point to enhance your recovery process.

- Keep your thoughts about the body part and your health positive and about healing.
- If you find yourself thinking negatively or doubting your healing ability and health, stop the negative thoughts and replace them with positive thoughts based on facts.
- Avoid thinking of the body part as hurt, injured, bad, and so on. If you have these thoughts, stop them with your trigger or cue word, and change them to positive thoughts about your healing, followed by a healthy image.
- Stop thoughts about how the injury happened. Replace them with thoughts about your healing.
- Create affirmations regarding the healing, health, and strength of the body part. For example, try to keep thinking, *I am strong, healthy, recovered, healed, better than ever,* etc. Even if you still have a long way to go to recover, say affirmations to yourself about your desired end result.
- Say or think an affirmation every time you look at the body part, think of it, wash it, exercise, wake up, go to bed – all the time!
- Post notes of the affirmations everywhere.
- When you see the notes, read them, think them, and imagine them.

Activation control

Maintaining your optimal activation level throughout the healing process is essential. Tension can hinder your healing, especially if the area surrounding the injury experiences muscular tension. Therefore, it is extremely important to keep the area relaxed, particularly when getting treatment and exercising. In addition, complete relaxation will speed up your body's rejuvenation process, so that it has more energy to direct toward healing. You will also find that your favorite energizing techniques can help you increase your motivation and effort during physical therapy sessions. Use these helpful hints for relaxation and energizing:

- Relax the surrounding area by releasing the tension with focused ribcage breathing.
- Use the Colors imagery technique, and other imageries, to relax the area.
- Keep your focus and thoughts positive and soothing to relax the area.
- Use your favorite complete relaxation technique after receiving treatments or physical therapy and at the end of the day.
- If you feel tense before a treatment or physical therapy session, use a complete relaxation technique to reduce your activation level.
- If you feel your activation level drop during physical therapy, use your favorite energizing techniques to give yourself a boost of energy. Motivate yourself even more by focusing on the fact that every exercise will bring you closer to being healed.

Imagery

There have been numerous studies on the relationship between the use of imagery and enhanced rehabilitation. Cancer patients have had miraculous recoveries after using imagery along with medical treatment. Although several ideas follow, use your imagination to create other ways to use this effective mental skill.

- Imagine the body part healed.
- See the body part getting stronger when you receive treatment and during physical therapy. Ask questions to learn exactly what happens as it heals, so that you can create a realistic, detailed image.
- Pick a *healthy* color and an *injured* color. Imagine the body part surrounded by the injured color, and then see the healthy color overtake the area.

- Imagine and feel the warmth of healing blood surround the area, especially during treatment. If you're icing the area, imagine any swelling leaving the area.
- Imagine something inside you fixing the area, such as mini construction people, super-healer cartoons, special creatures, healing fairies, etc. Make the image very detailed.
- Imagine a healing beam of light flooding the area with healing energy.

Attentional focus

As is always the case, what you choose to focus your attention on will have an impact on your body. In general, your focus should be positive and remain on your body healing.

- Throughout the healing process, make sure that you thoroughly understand the desired effects of your therapy and any prescribed exercises. Keep an intense focus on the area of the body healing and getting stronger during therapy.
- If you find that your focus is on pain that is part of the healing process, use a distraction technique or one of the suggestions for dealing with pain in the next chapter to change your focus back to the healing process. If you aren't sure if the pain you are feeling is part of the healing process, consult a medical professional promptly.
- If you must talk about how the injury happened, follow your description with positive comments about your healing process.
- Focus on any progress you have made, instead of on how far you have to go to get back to top form. Every sign of healing is important.

Seek out others for further support

Try to use a combination of mental skills to enhance your healing. Do your best to stay strong throughout the rehabilitation process, and maintain a belief that you will heal quickly. In addition, find other athletes who have experienced what you are going through, or who are in a similar situation. Talking with and getting support from these people can be extremely helpful. Ask the medical professionals you are working with to get you in touch with such individuals. If you like the idea of being part of a group, some sports medicine facilities and universities have injured-athlete support groups that are led by local sport psychology professionals, as well. If you have to stay off the ice for a period of time, keep in touch with your coach(es) and skating friends to avoid feeling cut off from something you love.

Enhanced healing for team skaters

In addition to using the mental skills as suggested, it is important for any team skater to stay connected to his or her teammate(s) throughout the healing process. If you are unable to train for a period of time, be sure to observe training sessions whenever possible, attend all meetings, keep in contact with your coach(es) and your teammate(s), and participate in any social events.

How to use mental skills when you resume training

If your injury required you to alter your training, following the advice of the medical professionals regarding how soon to return – and at what pace – will be extremely important. Once you have healed and are ready to return to full training, the use of mental skills can help make the transition easier. Although the process can be frustrating, do your best to be kind and patient with yourself!

Goals. Set many daily goals as you regain your strength, timing, and form. Setting goals will enable you to experience success often, and it will keep your focus on your technique and progress.

Self-talk. Keep your self-talk positive and in the present. If you start thinking *what if something bad happens* and other fear-based thoughts, use a thought-stoppage technique immediately. Change these to thoughts based on facts about your progress, your strength, and information from your doctor. Stop thoughts of how the injury happened, and put yourself back in the present with positive thoughts of how you are now or what you can do to get back to top form. Say affirmations about your strength and progress several times every day.

Activation control. Release any tension you notice before you get on the ice and while you skate, especially if you feel afraid or frustrated with your body and rate of progress. Use your favorite complete relaxation techniques after you train and before you go to sleep each night to help the rejuvenation process. Depending on how your training was affected, you may need to build up your stamina again. Use your favorite energizing techniques to maintain your activation level while building up your strength.

Imagery. Imagine skating in top form to enhance your confidence level. If your level of skating is lower than it was before the injury, imagine how you accomplished each progression with your body previously. This will help remind your mind and body that each step is possible. Once this image is clear, go do it! Watch videos of yourself in top form to reconnect with that feeling. Make your imageries as realistic as possible, and always imagine yourself as fully healed.

Attentional focus. Keep your focus on your health and improvements. Depending on how your training was affected, you may need to have a more instructional focus for skills you would normally have done automatically, until your timing comes back. If you become fearful of reinjuring yourself, use a distraction technique to get rid of the fear, and refocus on what you are doing. Lastly, if you must describe your injury to someone, always follow the description with a positive statement regarding your health, strength, or progress.

Enhanced healing: final round

The best medicine for injury is prevention! Follow the periodization method for your on- and off-ice training, use quality technique, listen to your body, treat your body and mind well with good nutrition and proper rest, maintain your equipment, and follow the advice of your coach(es), parents, and medical professionals to avoid injury as best you can.

If you do get injured, remember that an essential aspect of a successful recovery is allowing your body time to heal. The biggest mistake most driven athletes make when dealing with an injury is pushing too hard by doing too much too soon. Listen to your body and follow the medical advice you are given to avoid letting your desire to return to top form rush your recovery. Use any down time you have from physically training to improve other skills and other areas of your life. For example, if you can't go to the arena to train for a while, use the same time to improve your mental skills. If you aren't allowed to do any cross training, you can spend the time reading biographies of great athletes and researching cutting-edge nutrition information and training techniques.

It is important to remember that resuming training after an injury can be accompanied by stress, frustration, and self-doubt. Make sure you surround yourself with supportive people, and be your own best friend throughout the process. At times you may need to be gentle and patient, while at other times you may need to be tough and push past unnecessary limitations you placed on yourself. Use your own experience and knowledge from others to decide what you need, and take responsibility to get and do what is best for you. Lastly, keep in mind that you can apply this same information to enhance healing associated with any illness, as well.

> *Something just clicked and I was in the zone for the seven weeks between Nationals and the Olympics. I focused on healing and on training.*
> **Nancy Kerrigan: Olympic & World Medalist, U.S. National Champion, on her successful comeback after being attacked and injured before the Olympics**

Message to coaches and parents

The best way to deal with injuries is to prevent them in the first place. If you're a coach, you are responsible to communicate to both students and parents the importance of skaters' using proper technique, training smart and sensibly both on and off the ice using the periodization method, warming up and cooling down before and after every training session, avoiding overtraining elements, listening to their bodies, using and properly maintaining appropriate equipment, and eating and sleeping well. If you're a parent, you are responsible to do what you can to make certain that your child follows the advice of the coach and medical professionals – as well as your own guidance, of course!

Take the time to get to know the medical professionals in your area who are familiar with sports medicine. Make an effort to build relationships with those you feel are the most knowledgeable and professional, and who can understand the physical demands of skating. If an injury does come up, do your best to make sure the skater is properly treated as soon as possible. Insist that the skater follow the advice of medical professionals in regard to treatment, the healing process, and, when a break from skating is required, how soon to resume training. It is common for skaters to rush the healing process, so encourage patience to ensure a full recovery. If a break from skating is necessary, try to keep the skater in contact with coach(es) and skating friends, as well as team members, if applicable.

Here's another design you can focus on
as you repeat the following affirmation
(or repeat an affirmation of your choosing).

I am mentally tough and a strong athlete.

Chapter 8

Control Pain with Mental Toughness

I believe you're capable of more than you ever think you are, and it's only when you're faced with a situation that really tests you that you realize what you can do.
**Nancy Kerrigan: Olympic & World Medalist,
U.S. National Champion**

As an athlete, you'll find that there are times during which you have to skate with pain. This does not mean that *no pain, no gain* is a good motto or that all pain should be ignored. The feeling of pain can be the body's way of telling you that something is very wrong and you should take immediate action (such as go see a medical expert!). However, there is another type of pain that is related to the healing process, and it can be worked through. You might experience this type of pain when you're returning from an injury, after a hard workout, or if you are fighting off a minor illness like a cold.

It is important to differentiate between *good pain* that you can work through and *bad pain* that requires immediate medical attention and/or rest. It is best to discuss how to tell the difference with your parents, coach, trainer, or doctor. Never, ever push through any pain unless you are sure it is the healing type of pain. Following are lists of several ways to use mental skills to deal with the good pain that can be safely ignored and worked through.

Self-talk

As with any other situation, when you're experiencing pain you want to keep your self-talk positive, focused on getting the task done, and simple. More specifically, do the following:

- Keep your self-talk positive and realistic in order to enhance your confidence in your ability to work through any pain.
- If you find that your self-talk is about your pain, use a trigger to interrupt your thoughts before thinking about how strong you are. If you are resuming training after an injury or it is a couple of days after a hard workout, remind yourself of your healing progress. Follow this up with thoughts related to your skating.
- If you went to see a medical professional, base your self-talk on what the doctor told you about the pain you are experiencing. For example, think about what the professional said concerning your healing, strength, ability to work through the pain, etc.

Activation control

Try out each of the following relaxation and energizing techniques to decrease the pain and maintain your optimal activation level:

- Relax any specific area of your body that is in pain as much as possible *without* squeezing the muscles. This is important because muscular tension often increases pain and slows the healing process.
- Before you step on the ice, as well as several times while you're on the ice, do a complete body scan and release any tension you find.
- Use focused ribcage breathing to maintain your optimal activation level, and think *in with strength, comfort, and/or health* as you inhale and *out with pain and weakness* as you exhale.

- If you feel like your pain is draining your energy, use your favorite energizing technique to pump up your energy level. Follow up by purposely focusing on what you are doing instead of how you are feeling.

Imagery

Try these imageries to discover which will work for dealing with your pain, or create your own.

- Imagine you have a switch on your body that can turn off pain, and use it!
- Imagine that the pain is outside your body and not a part of you. Detach yourself from the feeling of pain.
- Imagine the pain as a color surrounding the affected area, and change the color to one that represents a healthy, strong, comfortable feeling.
- Imagine a light beam with healing energy targeting the spot to make it heal and take away the pain.
- Imagine the area turning cold and clammy, then numb it, and have no feeling at all in that specific area.
- Imagine the pain getting smaller and smaller, until it completely disappears.
- Imagine the pain as a huge claw pinching the area; then imagine the claw loosening its grip.
- Imagine the pain as a vicious, evil animal, and imagine relief as a pack of strong, oversized dogs. Like a confrontation between good and evil, imagine the dogs challenging the evil animal until the evil animal shrinks away out of fear and turns into a puddle of water. Lastly, see the dogs lick up the puddle. With this, the good wins over the evil, and the pain is taken away.
- Imagine a vacuum inside the area sucking up the pain.
- Imagine that you are sitting on a chair in the middle of a stadium, and picture your favorite people sitting in the bleachers surrounding you. These special people are there to send you positive, healing energy and to take away any pain that you are feeling.
- Imagine anything that takes the pain away!

Attentional focus

If your focus is on your pain, use one of the distraction techniques you have learned to change your focus. Keep the following points in mind, as well:

- Change your focus from the pain to feelings of healing and strength, healthy thoughts, past experiences when you felt strong, enjoyable things, and/or technical cues if you are on the ice. For example, if you are skating and feel pain, take a moment to do a ribcage breath to release the pain and change your focus to how strong the rest of your body feels. Say an affirmation, such as *I feel as strong as ever,* and return your focus to what you are working on at the time.
- Change your focus from what you are feeling to what you are doing.
- Change your perception of the feeling. Instead of labeling the sensation as *pain,* think of it as a warm, dull feeling that is neither positive nor negative.

Dealing with pain: final round

Testing your limits is important to the development of your Inner Champion. You will never know how tough you really are if you always allow good pain to sideline your training. Backing away from this sort of challenge will also cause you to miss out on valuable practice time, and you will have no experience to fall back on if faced with pain at a crucial moment. For example, if you have already proven to yourself that you are tough enough to work through something like a cold or muscle strain during practice, you will have confidence if you ever have to deal with a similar situation during an event.

However, no matter how tough you are, it is critical that you understand the difference between the pain you can work through and the pain that needs prompt medical attention and/or rest. If you have any doubt about pain you are experiencing, talk to your coach or parent and consult a medical professional as soon as possible!

Message to coaches and parents

Make certain that you discuss with your students or child the difference between pain that can be worked through and pain that needs to be listened to and dealt with accordingly. It is important that coaches and parents learn the delicate balance between overreacting and inaction; although if you're unsure, it is always better to be safe than sorry when dealing with the health of your students or child. Establish a relationship with sport medicine professionals in your area, including an orthopedic physician and a physical therapist who are knowledgeable in the field.

If it seems that your student or child is using pain as a way to avoid skating, immediately discuss this issue with the skater and the other core members of the skater's Inner Champion Circle. This type of avoidance behavior is usually a sign that there is a serious problem with the current situation, and it should be addressed as soon as possible. If the skater will not open up about your concerns with you or another member of the Inner Champion Circle, seek out a sport psychology professional to discuss the issue with the skater. Professional intervention is highly recommended for the well-being of the skater and is more than worth the time, effort, and money it will take.

Here's another design you can focus on
as you repeat the following affirmation
(or repeat an affirmation of your choosing).

I skate my best and have fun when I perform.

Chapter 9

Perform Like an Inner Champion

> *Just skate for yourself, no matter who is competing. It's just you and the ice. . . . Skate from the heart. To win is good, to skate well is even better.*
> **Michelle Kwan: the most decorated U.S. female skater**

You can control your ability to perform your best on a consistent basis – you just have to choose to do the things that will give you that control. Perhaps most important, you will need to create a specific approach for preparing both mentally and physically for events, as well as have a clear plan to follow during and after events. Although numerous strategies regarding the use of mental skills for events are included throughout the manual, this chapter provides an overview to help you design an effective method of preparation and plan of action. Remember that these are only suggestions and that you, along with your Inner Champion Circle, must discover what works best for bringing out your Inner Champion performances. If you skate on a team, all the core members of the team's Inner Champion Circle should create the team's method of preparation and plan of action together.

Preparation for events

Your mental and physical preparation is your best defense when performing under pressure. Preparation leads to consistency, consistency leads to confidence, and confidence leads to being able to handle pressure and skate with success. However, a lack of preparation will likely result in self-doubt and, most often, a poor performance.

There are many things in skating that you can't control, but you can control how prepared you are, both mentally and physically, for every event. For example, each practice can either help or hurt your potential to reach your performance goals for the season, so being prepared requires you to use your practice time wisely. In addition, you can ignore the mental side of your sport, or you can better prepare by training your mental skills as intensely as your physical skills. You also need to make good nutrition, healthy sleep patterns, and having downtime to play and rest priorities to be properly prepared to achieve success.

Practice with a purpose. Your training time provides the best opportunity to do most of your mental and physical preparation. Your coach(es) should tell you how to use your training time to best prepare yourself, but you alone are responsible for the quality of your training. Take this responsibility seriously by always practicing with a purpose if you want to be able to perform like an Inner Champion.

The purpose of practice when preparing for an event is simple – train how you want to perform so that events can feel more like practice. If you skate how you want to perform numerous times before an event, you will be able to feel comfortable and confident at events instead of feeling unfamiliar, full of doubt, and stressed out. Nothing feels better as you are waiting for your name to be announced than knowing you have done more clean run-throughs than you can count!

Expecting to perform in a way that you have never practiced is unrealistic and a sure way to set yourself up for disappointment. Training aimlessly, carelessly going through the motions, and avoiding complete run-throughs just wastes precious practice time and does nothing to enhance your preparation. Avoid these mistakes by making every movement count, and commit to bringing high energy to your training.

Increase the pressure you feel before every performance run-through by imagining you are at the location of your next event. Imagine you are skating in front of judges and/or an audience, and demand the mental and physical intensity of a performance.

> By making every practice as important as a competition, your body will know just what to do when the time comes, and that feeling will give you confidence to skate your best.
> **Members of the Haydenettes:**
> **U.S. National Synchronized Champions**

Create consequences for the quality of your skating to increase the pressure you feel even more. For example, reward a good run-through by spending extra time at the end of a session practicing fun tricks you want to add to your repertoire. A poor skate can result in skating extra laps to improve your stamina or working on an element (or exercise) that is important but is not a favorite of yours to practice. Making a mistake in a program shouldn't necessarily be regarded as a poor skate if you keep going and are able to change your focus to make the remaining elements your best. Every day can take you one step closer or one step farther from your goals and dreams. The sooner you realize that wasting training time is like giving away a little bit of your dream, the sooner you will be able to make your dreams come true!

Practice dealing with mistakes. An important aspect of preparation involves dealing with mistakes as if you are performing every day you train. Make it a habit to finish everything you start when drilling elements and skating performance run-throughs. If you fall on a jump, get up as quickly as you can and hit a checkout position; if you trip during connecting steps, footwork, a field move, or a dance pattern, pick up the steps as soon as possible and finish the pattern; if you lose your balance on a spin, lift, or anything else, do your best to regain your composure and keep going.

After each recovery within a performance run-through, change your focus to the next element, and then evaluate what went wrong when you are finished. If you normally stop and start over after making a mistake in the middle of a performance run-through, take action to break this bad habit immediately. This behavior does little to prepare you for an event because you will never be able to start over during a performance (unless you have a serious problem and the referee blows the whistle). When you're doing a performance run-through, keep going unless you seriously hurt yourself, have an equipment failure, or will injure someone in the way of your pattern. Doing so will allow you to practice letting mistakes go and refocusing on the remaining elements one at a time. This type of preparation will help you gain confidence to perform no matter what happens.

Another bad habit is to sit or lie on the ice after a fall and then only slowly get up. If you ordinarily do this, you can't expect to all of a sudden be able to bounce back up and resume the flow of your performance when you are at an event. You will be able to deal with a fall the best way possible if you practice your mental and physical response each time you fall in practice. Remember that the faster you get up, the sooner you can share all of the other things you are capable of doing. The only time you should sit on the ice is when you are seriously injured and need help to get off the ice.

Prepare for changes in schedules and altitude. Once you know the time of day you will skate, consider skating at that time for a few days if it is extremely different from your practice schedule. For example, if you must perform late at night and you always train early in the morning, you may want to skate at night for a few days before the event. If you know you will need to change your sleep schedule for the event, you may want to initiate the changes a few days early to make the adjustment easier. If you need to prepare for jetlag and altitude changes, research the latest information on how to deal with these issues and follow the current suggestions.

Skate a mock event. Participating in a mock performance can be a highly effective tool when preparing for an event. Skating clubs will often organize an exhibition or judge critique before an event. Approach such experiences as if you are really performing at the actual event. If a mock event is not possible, use a practice session to simulate your performance. Wear what you've decided to use for the event, go through the on- and off-ice warm-up routine you plan to do, and perform your program, dance, or moves. Treat the performance as if it is the real event. Whether you skate an exhibition, critique, or practice session, take notes afterward. List the things you want to repeat for the actual event and what changes you want to make. Include mental and physical aspects in your notes, and then use what you learned when the event takes place.

Set event goals. Write your goals for the event in your mental toughness training journal at least one month before the performance date. Make them SMART and Positive, and include both mental and physical aspects of your skating. Start with the goals to have fun while challenging yourself to skate your best and to enjoy your performance. If you are part of a team, make certain your goals support the goals of your team.

Stay focused on your goals by reviewing them each week as the event approaches. Set daily goals that will bring you closer and closer to achieving your event goals, and take action every practice to achieve them. Maintain your motivation level by writing affirmations for your goals and post them everywhere. Further increase your motivation and confidence by doing daily imageries of achieving your goals before you practice and at the end of the day.

Think like an Inner Champion. Stay aware of your self-talk, and use the various techniques you have learned to keep it positive and focused on what you want to do. Be prepared to use self-talk control techniques off the ice more often as the event approaches. You can increase your confidence level by writing as many affirmations as you can think of in your mental toughness training journal. Post the affirmations around your home and take the time to imagine what you read. A great way for a team to prepare for an event and boost confidence is to use team mottoes or affirmations decided on by all team members.

It will be easier to think like an Inner Champion if you keep the upcoming event in perspective. If you are worried or fearful about your next performance, interpret your emotions as a sign that you need to change your perspective of the situation. View events as a chance to have fun challenging yourself to excel. It is also an opportunity to share your love of skating and the improvements you have made with those watching.

Control your activation level. Be alert for signs that you need to adjust your activation level on and off the ice. You may need to energize yourself if additional hours are added to your training schedule, if your practice ice is later or earlier than you are accustomed to, or if you need to travel to the event. Think of possible stressors and energy zappers you might experience during the event, and choose the techniques you will use to deal with each one. Be prepared to deal with unknown stressors and energy zappers, as well. Remember to use a technique for complete relaxation if you have any trouble sleeping before the event.

Use your imagination. Imagine you are skating at the event location each time you train your performance. If you have been to the location before, imagine as many details of the ice and the surroundings as you can to increase your comfort level during the event. In the weeks before the event, take time to imagine your best performance not only before each practice, but also at the end of every day. Do both the full-length and short versions of performance imagery. Include as many details specific to the event and its location as possible.

If you have never been to the arena, imagine a generic ice surface until you arrive at the site of the event. Once you arrive at the arena, take notice of where you will be entering and exiting the ice, where the judges and audience will be sitting, the lighting, the sound quality of the music and announcements, and the temperature of the rink. Add these details and anything else you notice to your final imageries.

Stay focused. Keep your focus in the present and on your goals, the proper technique, the positives, and what is under your control while you prepare for each event. As you get closer to the day of the event, focus on your strengths and progress instead of any weaknesses. This is not the time to focus on what you wish you would have fixed or learned by then, because you no longer have time to change things! You can focus on these things after the event when it's time to think about how you want to improve yourself.

Decide on the focus you desire throughout the event and write about it in your mental toughness training journal. Use this type of focus while you are training for the event to make your practice and performance as similar as possible. Further prepare yourself by writing down possible distractions you may experience during the event. Once the list is complete, decide on the techniques you will use to deal with the distractions. Add a description of the techniques to your list, and include a plan for dealing with unexpected distractions.

Avoid placing importance on who is in your group. Your ability to skate your best will not change if the current Olympic champion or someone in rental skates is in your group – unless you lose your focus by being distracted by your competitors. Stay focused on the fact that you are skating *with* the others in your group and *against* yourself as you challenge yourself to do your best. This is an especially useful perspective to maintain if you are in the same group as one or more of your friends. Likewise, focusing on whom you can or can't beat once groups are posted will rob you of mental and physical energy that can be better used when you focus on doing your best.

> *What game are you playing? Are you playing your best game or to best someone else?*
> **Kathy Casey: Olympic, World & National Coach**

If you skate practice ice, keep your focus on yourself, your coach(es), and your partner or team if applicable. If your focus starts to include the other skaters or teams or even people in the audience, remind yourself that you only have control of your skating and refocus on what *you* are doing. Remember that how others skate during practice, warm-up, or a performance has no effect on how you skate unless you let them and their skating distract you.

Another potential distraction is the order you draw to skate. The order you skate at an event will not determine how well you skate unless you place undue importance on it. There are positive and negative aspects to every skating position, so the best you can do is to focus on the good points and deal with any potential drawbacks to avoid being negatively affected. For example, when skating first, focus on the fact that you can go straight from the warm-up to your performance and keep the feel of the ice. However, you must do a shorter warm-up if you want to rest before you perform and quickly get your mind ready for your performance. In contrast, by skating last you can focus on having plenty of time to catch your breath, retie your skates, and do success imageries, but you must keep your body warm off the ice before you perform. You will increase your confidence in being able to skate well in any position by practicing your warm-up and performance with a variety of waiting periods.

Make a preparation checklist. In addition to training your mind and body, make a detailed checklist of things that need to be taken care of before the event and things you need to bring to the event. Make the list as complete as you can to avoid the anxiety of discovering that you forgot something when it comes time to perform! It is also a good idea if you or someone in your Inner Champion Circle takes care of the checklist items early, because waiting until the last minute to deal with these details can cause unnecessary stress for everyone. For example, travel plans; packing; taping skates; organizing extra laces, outfits, and tights or socks; and buying special food you like can all be taken care of ahead of time.

Plan of action during events

Develop a pre-performance routine that you can follow the day of an event. Following the same plan of action for each event can give you a sense of comfort, calmness, and confidence, as well as strengthen your consistency. Most important, as you complete your pre-performance routine, it will provide a signal to your mind and body that it is time to perform. It is important to realize that a pre-performance routine is different from superstitious rituals. Superstitious rituals focus on some sort of power that is not under your control, whereas a pre-performance routine is something you can do at every event to prepare your mind and body to perform. Be consistent with when and how you address the following details:

- How much you sleep the night before you perform and the length of any naps you take the day you perform.
- What and when you eat the night before you perform and during the event.
- The time you arrive at the building (avoid rushing so you can stay calm and focused).
- When to say good-bye to family and supporters and leave them to prepare.
- When and how you do your off-ice warm-up.
- The order and timing of getting ready (getting dressed, putting on skates, etc.).
- What you do during your on-ice warm-up.
- What you do during the time between the on ice-warm up and your performance.
- Anything else that you do before you perform.
- When and how you integrate your mental skills into your pre-performance routine.

Although you want to develop a pre-performance routine, you also need to be flexible for the unpredictable things that may happen. For example, the skater before you may withdraw seconds before he or she is supposed to skate, or the schedule may change. No matter what happens, remember that the only thing you have control of is yourself and your response to the unexpected.

Goals. Pick a time to read your goals on the day you skate to keep focused, motivated, and confident. If you start to have doubts, get distracted by the other skaters, or get tired, remind yourself of why you are there and that you are prepared for success! Replay your success imageries of your goals if you feel your confidence needs a boost.

> *At competitions, . . . I just try to stay as focused as I can on my goals [and] try to go out on the ice and skate as well as I can.*
> **Timothy Goebel: Olympic & World Medalist,
> U.S. National Champion**

Self-talk. Keep the event in perspective, and talk to yourself as you would to your best friend before, during, and after the event. Keep your thoughts encouraging and focused on what you are there to do, while you stop and replace any stinking thinking. Say your list of affirmations to yourself often, and think about how prepared you are. If you start to worry about any of your elements, remind yourself of how many times you have completed that element during practice. Chances are you will not be able to come up with an exact number because you have done it so many times. This is comforting knowledge since you need to do each element only one time during your performance.

Think of technical and/or encouraging thoughts during your on-ice warm-up, and think of more affirmations while you wait to perform. As your name is announced and you skate to your starting position, take a ribcage breath and think a positive thought. Throughout your performance, keep your thoughts as you would during a great practice. Some skaters do best when they quiet their minds and allow their bodies to do what they have been trained to do, and other skaters prefer to fill their minds with technical thoughts to block out anything else. It doesn't matter what approach you take, as long as it works for you and you are consistent with your thoughts in practice and performances.

A common mistake many skaters make is to think that the way they skate during their on-ice warm-up will determine how they skate when it is their time to perform. Some skaters think that a bad warm-up means a bad performance will follow, some think that a good warm-up means a bad performance will follow, and some think that they can perform well only if the entire warm-up is wonderful. If you start to think this way, stop the stinking thinking immediately! Your warm-up is just that, A WARM-UP! Of course a clean warm-up is desirable, but a warm-up full of misses doesn't mean your performance is doomed. Just because you miss elements in your warm-up doesn't mean you will miss them during your performance. This simply reflects that you were warming up your mind and body, and more importantly, that you made mistakes that you can correct during the performance.

> **Paul Wylie** provides an excellent example of how a not-so-perfect warm-up can lead to a stellar performance when you stay mentally tough. As noted previously, Paul's triple axel combination was one of his most difficult elements to perform, and during the warm-up for his short program at the Olympics, he missed both attempts of the combination. After the warm-up, Paul's coach calmly reminded him of the proper technique. Paul listened closely to his coach and then imagined himself doing the combination correctly. Next Paul remembered other competitions when he didn't land the combination in warm-up but nailed it during his performance. He also breathed deeply to help him relax and thought about all the times he landed the combination in practice.
>
> Paul felt nervous, but he also felt he could do it. He remembers that on the backward edge into the combination he had only one word on his mind – TRUST. Paul explained that he had to trust his training, trust his technique, and trust in God. He thought through every step of his program and focused on one element at a time. Paul skated a clean short program that day, and he kept up his top form and mental toughness to go on to win the Olympic silver medal.

If you have a poor warm-up, take time before you perform to clear your mind of the mistakes you made and review the correct technique. Follow this up with an imagery of performing your best. Finally, use a relaxation technique if you need to, and fill your mind with helpful thoughts before you take the ice to perform. Think of your technique as well as the number of times in your life you have been successful doing each element in your performance. Then skate out to your starting position knowing that you are ready to perform your best and enjoy the experience.

Unfortunately, some skaters think they need a poor warm-up to perform great because they have had past experiences when their warm-up was awful but their performance was awesome. These skaters actually get really nervous if they warm up well! If you think about your warm-up this way, change your thinking so you stop believing your warm-up controlled your performance. Instead, realize you performed so well because you were able to refocus after your poor warm-up and made the necessary corrections during your performance. If you do this, you will be able to enjoy a good warm-up and put yourself back in control of your performance.

Activation control. Check in with your activation level throughout the day of your performance and make any needed adjustments. Work this into your pre-performance routine to make it a natural thing to do. Be sure to check in with your body and mind during your off-ice warm-up; while you put on your skates; before, during, and after your on-ice warm-up; and while you wait to perform. Use the techniques you chose as part of your preparation to make adjustments. Before your performance begins, take a deep ribcage breath while thinking a positive thought. Continue to ribcage breathe throughout the performance, and make quick adjustments if needed. Remember that your thoughts, emotions, focus, and breathing can affect your activation level.

Imagery. Do a long-version imagery the night before and/or the day of your performance, and do at least one short version right before you perform. If you skate first or second, imagine both your on-ice warm-up and the performance before the on-ice warm-up. Otherwise, imagine the on-ice warm-up before, and the performance after, your on-ice warm-up. Remember to include the details of the building, your clothes, the ice, and the crowd, as well as how you want to feel, what you want to think, and what you want to focus on throughout the imagery.

Attentional focus. Keep your focus on your skating, your strengths, and enjoying yourself! Change your focus if it is on anything other than the present, the positives, what you have control of, and what you want to do. Be prepared to use the techniques you previously decided would work for you to deal with any distractions.

To avoid having regrets after your performance, let yourself go and skate from your heart, knowing you have everything to gain and nothing to lose. Clear your mind of doubts, fears, judgments, pressure, and the expectations of others, so that you can skate freely with intensity. Instead of skating with hope, trust your preparation and skate with confidence. Command the ice with your presence, attack your performance, and expect the best from yourself. Focus on the belief that when you step on the ice to perform, it is your time to shine!

> Anything you do in your career can never be taken away from you. Every day is new and whatever you accomplish only adds to what you've done in the past. So you can't lose; you can only gain.
> **Janet Lynn: Olympic Medalist &
> U.S. National Champion**

Plan of action when events are over

Remember how you felt when you got off the ice, regardless of the marks you received or the reaction of the audience. If you skate great and receive high marks, view the marks and possible medal as a bonus to the real reward of knowing you prepared well and gave everything you had to your performance. If you skate poorly, but get good marks, be thankful that your good qualities weren't completely overshadowed by your mistakes. However, still take a good look at what happened so you can avoid making the same mistakes again. If you skate a wonderful performance, but get low marks, don't let the opinions of the judges spoil your happiness and satisfaction in knowing you did your best.

> It doesn't matter how we placed. I think we did a remarkable program for ourselves. . . . The judges [will] never be able to take the feeling away that we were able to feel this night. I'll take this with me the rest of my life – a feeling of accomplishment.
> **John Zimmerman: Olympian, World Pair Medalist
> & U.S. National Pair Champion on his
> Olympic freeskate with Kyoko Ina**

After each event, evaluate what did and did not work for both your method of preparation and your plan of action. Use your mental toughness training journal to write about what you achieved and learned. You will be able to better prepare yourself for the next event if you have these notes to consult. Be consistent in your approach, yet realize that as you gain experience and mature, you may need to update your method of preparation and your plan of action.

In terms of mental skills, go over what you were thinking. Which thoughts made you feel the best? Did anything make it easy to doubt yourself? Include in your evaluation how you were able to control your activation level and focus. Of course, you should also write about the physical aspects and other details that you would like to repeat or change in the future. After a great performance, imagine the experience a few times later that day to encode it into your memory. Then you can use the memory as a success imagery in the future. If you had a poor performance, only imagine the experience a few times to get ideas of what you can do differently the next time, and then move on from the experience.

Always review your goals after you skate. Celebrate your successes, and discover the lessons you can learn when you don't achieve all of your goals. How did you feel when your performance was over? Were you proud, satisfied with your efforts, and completely exhilarated? Did you have fun and give everything you had to offer to your performance? Did you feel regret and wish you could go do it again? If you did not achieve your goals, ask yourself if they were realistic. Did you do your best to prepare yourself? Did you just get out-skated, or were the standards higher than you expected? Did you lose your focus and confidence or get too nervous, never regaining your desired activation level? Can you do anything differently to improve your performance for the next event?

> I always turned a bad skate into something good. It made me determined never to make the same mistake again, and I couldn't wait for the next opportunity to show how I could really skate.
> **Elaine Zayak: Olympian, World & U.S. National Champion**

It is important to determine what happened so you can learn from the experience. Naturally, you may feel discouraged or disappointed after a poor performance. However, dwelling on such feelings will not help you skate better the next chance you have. Try to keep in mind that the sooner you learn the lessons from the experience and move on, the better it will be for your next performance. Lastly, evaluate your Inner Champion Circle and your teammates, if appropriate. Meet with the core of your Inner Champion Circle to discuss what worked and what needs to be changed for the next event. This meeting will help make the next event a positive experience for everyone.

Inner Champion performance: final round

Take charge of each performance by doing everything in your power to bring out your best. Many talented skaters fail to reach their potential due to their lazy training habits, weak mental skills, and overall lack of preparation. Other very successful skaters make up for what they lack in natural talent with an excellent work ethic, the consistent use of mental skills, and systematic preparation for events. If you want to make the most of your talents, be sure to prepare yourself for every event as well as possible and follow your plan of action. Your hard work, mental toughness, and thorough preparation will allow you to know in your mind and feel in your body that it is your time to shine every time you step on the ice to perform.

Once you realize that performing well is under your control and no longer about being lucky, it will be easier to feel excited about every event. To fully enjoy each performance, skate because you love it, have fun while you compete against yourself, and put all that you can – your heart, your soul, your full effort – into every performance.

Message to coaches and parents

Coaches:

Promote the goal to *practice with a purpose* every day. Encourage your students to practice how they want to perform so events can feel more like practice. Ask your students to imagine they are performing at their next event every time they skate a performance run-through. Avoid stopping and starting music once a program or dance is memorized to help your students learn how to follow through from beginning to the end. Explain that they should pause or stop during a performance run-through only if they seriously injure themselves, experience equipment failure, or will endanger another skater by staying on pattern. If you use double run-throughs as a training technique, emphasize to your students that the purpose of the drill is to build their endurance and confidence. However, make it very clear that they shouldn't treat the second run-through as a second chance to make up for a poor first attempt, since they will never have such an opportunity at an event.

Conduct yourself in the same manner throughout the season because your students will be sensitive to changes in your behavior and attitude. Many coaches get extremely tense right before an event, while others become very distant. This sort of change in behavior can be an additional source of stress to skaters. You can make practice more like a performance for your students by bringing the same sort of positive energy to both situations. If you want consistency from your skaters, you must be consistent yourself.

> As coaches, we must be aware of our attitudes and behavior at competition times so that we do not change from our normal patterns. Even a change in appearance can be distracting to your students, such as wearing bright colors at competition if you only wear black to practice every day.
> **Christy Ness: Olympic, World & National Coach**

Be sure to prepare students and parents who are new to the skating world by explaining what to expect at different events. Even seasoned skaters and parents will benefit from additional guidance before their first national and international competitions. If you are taking a student to an event that is also new for you, contact others who have experience at similar events to discover what you and your skater can expect. Help your students create an event preparation checklist, and orchestrate mock events throughout the season. Allow your students to gain the understanding that judges are ordinary people with a love for skating, rather than people who should be feared, by introducing skaters to judges during critiques or club events.

> *Our coach, Mr. Nicks, knew how to train us. We knew exactly what to expect at competitions, and we knew exactly what to do when we stepped on the ice – that gave us a lot of confidence.*
> **Ken Shelley: Olympian, World Pair Medalist, U.S. National Champion & U.S. National Pair Champion with JoJo Starbuck**

Discuss the goals of each student or team before every event, and encourage a focus on things under their control. Remind your students and their parents of your definition of success as it relates to winning versus having fun striving to win and skating your personal best. On the day of the performance, allow time for imageries if your students have mastered this skill. Call attention to how well prepared and trained your students are before they perform, and remind your students to think of their affirmations.

Be aware of the optimal activation level for each of your students, and help them make adjustments if needed. If they seem nervous, stressed, worried, or tense, ask them to do their favorite relaxation exercise. Remind them that a little bit of extra energy is a good sign that their mind and body are getting ready to perform, and suggest that they focus on how ready and able they are to skate well. Stay aware of your own optimal activation level, as well, and make any necessary adjustments. Events can be stressful for coaches, so pace yourself to be able to be at your best throughout an entire event.

When reviewing a performance immediately after a student skates, be sensitive to the fact that this is an exceptionally vulnerable time for most skaters. Focus on the positives as much as possible by sandwiching critiques with praise. Follow the lead of your students in regard to the depth of your discussion at this time. If your students performed well, you will have plenty to talk about right away. However, sometimes there aren't many positives, and you may be able to point out only that the skater kept going despite missing every element in the program. In this case, it is best to save a complete evaluation until later.

> Teach your students the invaluable rewards of striving to be their best no matter what they do. Be honest with evaluations, but leave them with their heads held high.
> **JoJo Starbuck: Olympian, World Pair Medalist & U.S. National Pair Champion with Ken Shelley**

Remind your students to evaluate themselves and their Inner Champion Circle after every event so they can continuously learn and grow from their successes and disappointments. Evaluate events as well, and if you don't like the outcome of an event, decide the best way to change the process for a better chance of success the next time. Your evaluation should include taking a look at the effect you have on your students and teams. If you are uncertain of your effectiveness, ask your students to give you an honest evaluation to help improve your performance as a coach. Discuss complete evaluations with your students, their parents, and other members of the Inner Champion Circle, as appropriate, soon after each event. Everyone should openly discuss what should stay the same, and what should change, and then agree on a plan to move forward.

No matter how bad the skating, it is extremely important that you don't allow your ego to get in the way of supporting your student after a poor performance. Walking away from the rail or giving the silent treatment after a poor performance can do irreparable damage to a skater's psyche and the coach-student relationship. It is rare for people to purposely sabotage their success or humiliate themselves in front of a crowd, and it is highly unlikely that a poor performance was motivated by a desire to embarrass someone else (such as a coach). Avoid punishing your students and treating them as if their failures are a personal assault on you while you work through your own disappointment.

*If a team does well, they don't **need** the coach around after the skate. If the team does not have a good skate, the coach **needs** to stick around to give perspective to the situation and not allow them to dwell on the negatives. They need to get motivated to make the next performance a satisfying one!*
Lynn Benson: World & National Coach

However, if you have an issue with a student's poor behavior as opposed to a poor performance – such as blatantly disrespecting you, the judges, or other skaters by acting inappropriately on or off the ice during the event – you should definitely deal with the behavior accordingly. Lastly, keep each event in perspective, remember that a little humor can help ease even the most stressful or disappointing situation, and never lose sight of the mission statement of each student.

Parents:

Creating too much pressure to perform, pushing instead of encouraging, over-identifying with your child's successes and failures, giving attention or love based on the quality of a performance, and putting an emphasis on winning (or placing higher than specific skaters) are all ways to sabotage your child's performance. Be certain that you are supporting the mission statement of your child before, during, and after events.

Emphasize your child's strengths before an event, support a focus on what your child can control, and do what you can to help your child maintain an optimal activation level. Avoid strong reactions – positive or negative – once competition groups are posted. Remind your child and yourself that successful competitors skate with, and not against, the others in their group as they compete against their own personal best. You may need to emphasize this perspective more than usual the first few times your child is put in a group with skaters who are also his or her friends.

Allow your child time and space to get focused on his or her performance, and help other family members and friends understand the importance of doing so, too. Keep your behavior and attitude consistent during practice and events, and use your favorite relaxation technique if you feel stressed or nervous before your child skates. If you have trouble controlling your nerves, give your child extra space to avoid letting your nerves cause unnecessary stress. If you are so nervous that you can't even watch your child perform, learn relaxation techniques to overcome your nerves. It will be worth the effort, because you rob yourself of a wonderful experience by not watching your child, and your inability to deal with the event sends a negative message to your child about performing.

> *You don't want your nerves or expectations to be a burden for your skater. At competition [Kristi and Christy] had their own pre-competition regime, and my role in the three-way partnership was elsewhere as a fan and spectator.*
> **Carole Yamaguchi: Mother of Olympic, World & National Champion Kristi Yamaguchi**

Treat your child the same way regardless of his or her performance. This will allow your child to feel that your love is not attached to skating. If your child performs well and places low, ask your child to think about how he or she felt immediately after the performance. Focus on the performance, and encourage your child to place more importance on what makes him or her feel proud instead of the opinion of the judges. If your child performs poorly, acknowledge the disappointment as well as the lessons that can be learned. Always evaluate the role you played in the success or failure of an event, and repeat what worked and change what did not!

Teach your child the value of good sportsmanship at competitions by being supportive of all the skaters in your child's group as well as the other skaters from your club or country. Make it a habit for you and your child to congratulate the top skaters in his or her group, no matter where your child is placed in the standings. Celebrate performances more than results, and most important, keep skating – and the significance of the event in relationship to life – in perspective! Remember that each event is one step in a long journey, and enjoy watching the development of your child's Inner Champion during every performance.

Mental Toughness Training Exercises

Make an event preparation checklist

Make a list of the things that you need to bring, do, buy, borrow, find, and organize before every event. Keep this list in your mental toughness training journal, and check off the various items as you (or your parent, coach, or someone you trust) take care of each detail. If you are new at testing, competing, or performing, ask your coach for guidance. Try to get organized early so that you don't cause yourself unnecessary stress at the last minute.

Take part in a mock event

Try to participate in a mock event. If an exhibition or critique is not possible, use a practice session or private ice. Be sure to wear what you plan to use for the event, and prepare yourself mentally and physically as if it were the real thing. After going through your planned preparation, including your off- and on-ice warm-ups, skate your performance as if you were at the actual event.

On the same day, evaluate what went well for you and what you would like to do differently for the actual performance. Focus on things that are under your control, and include both physical and mental aspects. Write your evaluation in your mental toughness training journal, and use this information as a guide to bring out your best when you go to the event.

If you are part of a team, you should have already discussed how best to prepare for the event. After the mock event, discuss with each other what did and did not work for the team members as individuals and as a team. Decide as a team if there are any changes that need to be made.

Whether you are a single or team skater, be sure to include the following questions in your evaluation.

1. What did not work while you were preparing, and how should you change this for the event?
2. What did work while you were preparing that you want to repeat for the event?
3. How did your pre-performance routine work for you?
4. What did not work while you were skating, and how should you change this for the event?
5. What did work while you were skating that you want to repeat for the event?

Remember to look at both mental and physical aspects, as well as how other people in your Inner Champion Circle (and teammates if appropriate) contributed to the success or failure of the mock event.

Set goals for events

Create at least three SMART and Positive goals for each event. Write your goals and the corresponding affirmations in your mental toughness training journal at least one month before the event. Post affirmations for each goal around your room or home, and imagine achieving your goals each time you think of them. If you are staying in a hotel for the event, have fun posting affirmations in your hotel room.

Review your goals each week leading up to the event, and set daily goals that support your event goals. Always record how well you did after each event. Celebrate your successes and write about what you learned if you did not reach your goals. Keep your goal sheets in your mental toughness training journal so you can keep track of your progress throughout the season and your career.

Put the event in perspective

Describe the perspective you would like to have in regard to what each event means to you and why you want to participate in it. Make sure your perspective supports your mission statement and your definition of success. Write this description in your mental toughness training journal, and read it if you feel yourself becoming stressed about the event.

Create event affirmations

Make a list of affirmations in your mental toughness training journal that includes as many positive statements as you can think of about yourself. Focus on your affirmations to get a confidence boost and to keep your Inner Champion perspective. Be sure to post them around your house or in your motel room if you need to travel to the event. If you are on a team, post both team and individual affirmations. Remind yourself of an affirmation if you start to feel nervous, distracted, tired, uncertain, etc. Think of an affirmation while you get dressed, lace your skates, wait to step on the ice, and take your starting position.

Prepare for stinking thinking

About two weeks prior to each event, create a list of any stinking thinking that might come up before and during your performance. Write the stinking thinking on the left side of a page in your mental toughness training journal, followed by the trigger or imagery you will use to stop each unwanted thought. Finish the list by writing a replacement thought on the right side of the page across from the original thought (make sure the replacement thoughts are positive, realistic, and focus on what is under your control). Review this list and use imagery to practice controlling your self-talk. If this exercise makes you feel more negative than prepared, skip it!

Plan for event stressors and energy zappers

Make a list in your mental toughness training journal of situations that could arise during each event that may cause you stress or zap your energy. Then pick a relaxation or energizing technique that you can use to control your reaction to the situation, and write the appropriate technique(s) next to each stressor or energy zapper. Use imagery to practice dealing with the potential stressors and energy zappers.

Use event imagery

Use your mental toughness training journal to keep track of the imageries you do before each event. Be sure to alternate long and short versions. Also alternate each phase of the event if you will be performing more than once. For example, if you have short, long, and artistic programs, or if you are a single skater and a team skater, alternate your imageries each day. Remember to include as many details as possible, and plan to do a full-length version the night before or the morning of your performance.

Describe your focus for the event

In your mental toughness training journal, describe the focus you desire throughout the entire event. Include such things as your goals, technique, your preparation, what is under your control, and staying in the present. Refer to your notes about your mock and actual events to refresh your memory about what works for you. What do you want to focus on during practice ice? Off-ice warm-up? On-ice warm-up? Between on-ice warm-up and your time to perform? During your performance?

Get ready to deal with event distractions

Make a list in your mental toughness training journal of possible distractions you may experience during the event. For each distraction, describe a distraction control technique you can use to stay properly focused. Refer to your notes or memory of past events to help you create this list. Describe how you would like to deal with unexpected distractions, as well. Use imagery to practice dealing with the possible distractions.

Establish a pre-performance routine

Describe the *what*, *when*, and *how* of your pre-performance routine. Incorporate both mental and physical aspects that will best prepare you to skate great. Include your sleep and wake-up schedule, eating that day, arriving at the rink, leaving your supporters, doing hair (and make-up if applicable), getting dressed, warming up off-ice, putting on your skates, what to do while waiting to take the ice for warm-up, warming up on the ice, what to do between warm-up and your performance, and the final moments when you step on the ice and are waiting to be announced. Also include time for imageries, checking in with your activation level, and thinking of affirmations and goals, as well as your desired focus. There's always a lot to do in preparation for your few minutes on the ice, but establishing a routine will make it easier to bring out your best at each event.

Conduct a post-event evaluation

After each event, conduct an evaluation to discover what did and did not work for your method of preparation and your plan of action. Title a page in your mental toughness training journal with the name of the event, write a general description of your experience, and answer the following questions. Complete your goal sheet for the event, as well. Refer to your event evaluations to help you prepare for your next event, and discuss your thoughts with the core members of your Inner Champion Circle.

1. **How did you skate?** Did you do your best? What was great about your performance? What could have been better? Did you have fun and enjoy the experience?
2. **What were you thinking about?** Describe the thoughts you remember having before, during, and after you skated. What thoughts helped you achieve your goals and what thoughts did not? Were you able to change any stinking thinking? What did and did not work? Did you focus on any affirmations? When and why? Did it seem to help you?
3. **What did you focus on before, during, and after you skated?** Do you feel that your focus helped you achieve your goals? Did you experience any distractions? Were you able to refocus? What did and did not work?
4. **Where was your activation level before, during, and after the event?** Did you feel yourself react to any stressors or energy zappers? Specifically what did you react to? Did you feel the need to make any adjustments? What

did you do to make any adjustments, and what did and did not work?
5. **Did you feel prepared for the competition?** Explain how you were and how you were not prepared. Did your imageries help you feel prepared? Did your training? How did your pre-event routine work for you? Did how you slept, ate, and spent your free time help or hurt you in reaching your goals? In the future, what would you do differently? What would you do the same?
6. **How did your Inner Champion Circle help or limit your efforts in reaching your goals?** What would you like them to repeat and to change? Did you thank them for their support and the role they played? While you evaluate your Inner Champion Circle, be sure that you don't blame others for things you control.
7. **Is there anything else you would like to remember about the experience?** Be sure to include any lessons you learned, what made you proud, your accomplishments, and any positive comments that were made about you.

Chapter 10

Make a Commitment to Be an Inner Champion

> *The most important thing is to love your sport. Never do it to please someone else. It has to be yours. That is all that will justify the hard work needed to achieve success.*
> **Peggy Fleming: Olympic, World & U.S. National Champion**

There are two characteristics that all Inner Champions possess: they skate for themselves and they skate for their love of the sport. As a result, they find it an easy choice to continuously apply their full effort and make the sacrifices necessary to turn their skating dreams into reality. Skating for yourself and because you love it will enable you to enjoy the process of striving to be your best, and it will make it easier to work through the challenges that all athletes face.

However, simply loving what you do will not ensure success – you must also take action. Most people want to be great, but very few are willing to do what it takes to achieve greatness. Inner Champions don't always feel like giving one hundred percent every day, but their passion and commitment to their mission provides the motivation to repeatedly push themselves to their healthy limits. Having passion and desire, a clear mission that excites you, and an inspiring dream isn't what will bring you to greatness. Putting your passion and desire *into action* to make your mission and dream a reality will!

> We love this sport more and more every year . . . and I think that's the key to success.
> **Tanith Belbin: World Junior Dance Champion & U.S. National Dance Champion with Ben Agosto**

Keep your passion for skating strong by never losing sight of your mission, and always skate for yourself. If you rarely enjoy skating or lack motivation and inspiration to achieve your goals and dreams, you can be sure you need to adjust how you and your Inner Champion Circle approach your skating.

Make a full-time commitment

This manual has explained specifically what it takes to be an Inner Champion. With this knowledge, you now have the choice to take complete responsibility for your skating experience by making a full-time commitment to developing your Inner Champion. You have read that your mind is a powerful tool that can either add or detract from your enjoyment, level of success, and overall love for skating. Dedicate the time and exert the energy to develop your mental toughness, and you will be able to take advantage of the amazing power of your mind. Apply yourself beyond just reading this manual by using mental skills consistently during practice, performances, and in other areas of your life. If you practice using these skills every day, you will find it easy to apply them during a performance under pressure.

> If your head is not in the right place, you can't do it. It doesn't matter how much you train.
> **Debi Thomas: Olympic Medalist, World & U.S. National Champion**

This manual has illustrated repeatedly how an untrained mind can negatively affect your performance – even when superb physical training habits and good technique are applied. However, as powerful as mental skills are, they can't take the place of physical training. No matter how mentally tough you are, you will still need to train hard physically on and off the ice to be the best you can be. It is also essential to keep in mind that being mentally tough involves more than mental skills training. Because your mind and body are connected, you must never discount the importance of fitness, nutrition, and sleep in your quest to be your best. Making a full-time commitment to developing your Inner Champion by focusing on both the mental and physical aspects of your training will enable you to make the most of your passion and dreams.

Continue your mental toughness training

Becoming mentally tough isn't quick or easy, but neither is mastering physical skills. It takes a lot of time, energy, and effort; yet the payoff is more than worth it! Reading this manual once and completing all of the exercises will help you, but you will benefit far more from rereading it and updating the exercises on an annual basis. As you grow and develop as a person and skater, you will understand the information differently each year. You will also find you are able to use some suggestions that didn't work for you in the past. This manual will be an invaluable tool throughout your entire skating career, but only if you use it consistently to take full advantage of its content!

Learn life lessons

Inner Champions often reach their potential in and out of the competitive arena, because they apply what they learn as an athlete to their life. Make an effort to use mental skills both on and off the ice, and you will improve your life in many ways. For example, you will be able to make the best of any situation that comes your way by taking control of what you can; you will be more optimistic, flexible, and focused; and you will be able to enjoy the moment as you strive to reach your goals off the ice. Think of mental skills as life skills that can be utilized every day. The more you use them, the more beneficial they become, especially in potentially stressful situations. Be creative in how you apply what you learn as a skater in all areas of your life!

> *If you enjoy your skating, no matter what the outcome or how much success you have, it will enrich your life. Skating can teach you many things that will help you throughout your life.*
> **Timothy Goebel: Olympic & World Medalist, U.S. National Champion**

Overcome challenges the Inner Champion way

If you commit to being an Inner Champion, you will experience far more highs than lows throughout your skating career. However, disappointment is a part of life, and no matter how well trained and mentally tough you are, you may experience some hard times. You might not reach all of your goals, some people may stop believing in you, and there may be days you feel like you can't do anything right or nothing will go your way.

Fortunately, you have discovered a variety of skills throughout this manual that will enable you to best control how you deal with these types of situations. Choose to perceive disappointments as temporary setbacks or challenges that you can overcome. Embrace the idea that a mistake is a failure only if you don't learn from it and neglect to move on to your next goal. Find the lesson each difficulty has to offer, remind yourself why you love skating, and then move on by refocusing on your mission and goals.

> *You will always have adversity to contend with in life. What we accomplished was because of sheer determination, our love for skating, and the support and guidance of our coaches and parents.*
>
> **Ken Shelley: Olympian, World Pair Medalist, U.S. National Champion & U.S. National Pair Champion with JoJo Starbuck**

Don't allow setbacks or other people's opinions to persuade you to let go of your passion for skating and give up. If you ever feel defeated, take a moment to think of Michael Jordan, one of the best basketball players of all time. Michael was cut from his high school basketball team and told he didn't have what it takes to make it as a basketball player. This came as quite a blow to Michael – one that would have caused many people to quit in order to avoid future disappointments. Fortunately, Michael didn't let that setback and the coach's opinion change his belief in himself and his dreams. Instead, he kept working on his game, continued to fuel his love of the sport, and ended up achieving amazing results! This inspiring story emphasizes the importance of staying true to yourself, your mission, and your love for skating, no matter what comes your way!

Make a commitment: final round

Very few athletes instinctively use mental skills without any formal training. In fact, nearly all people need to learn how to be mentally tough, and the manual you have just read provides the information you need to develop your Inner Champion and win the mental game. You have success at your fingertips with this manual – make a commitment to apply the information it contains and you will see just how incredible you can be as an Inner Champion!

Finally, perhaps the most important lesson you can learn is to be sure to love what you do and do what you love throughout your life. If you don't love skating and don't skate for yourself, it will be difficult to sustain the commitment and effort necessary to achieve excellence. Approach your skating with passion, make the most of your talent, and use mental toughness to enjoy the process of becoming the best you can be.

> *If I had never won a single medal, I'd still be skating in a rink somewhere. There wouldn't be an audience or camera flashes or autograph seekers – but I'd still be skating.*
> **Brian Boitano: Olympic, World & U.S. National Champion**

Message to coaches and parents

Never forget that you are essential to the success of your students and/or children. Make a commitment to continue developing the best methods to bring out the Inner Champion in your skater(s) and yourself!

Reread this manual throughout your career as a coach or parent, and consult the resource list at the back of the manual as a starting point to find additional sources of information for your continued education. There is always more you can learn, improve, and offer! The incredible journey of a life of excellence is worth the effort when you look at all of the wonderful experiences and joy that being an Inner Champion can bring.

> *I always loved teaching and [bringing] out the best in skaters. It takes drive, dedication, and understanding to be successful as an athlete and as a coach. . . . It's something I never get tired of, and I always want to keep getting better – my work is never done.*
> **Peter Burrows: Olympic, World & National Coach**

Mental Toughness Training Exercises

Rate your Inner Champion qualities

This exercise will help you become aware of how strong your Inner Champion qualities are at this point in time. When completing the exercise, be honest without being harsh, or easy, on yourself. For a well-rounded perspective, ask your coach, parents, and a skating friend to rate your Inner Champion qualities, as well. Explain that you want them to be honest, because their input will be useless if they tell you every quality is strong to avoid hurting your feelings when in reality you could work on some areas.

In your mental toughness training journal, write a numbered list from 1 to 50. Rate how each of the fifty statements below describes you right now by using the following percentages:

- 0% – That is not me at all.
- 1-50% – I'm very weak in this area.
- 51-70% – Somewhat describes me, but needs attention.
- 71-94% – Describes me most of the time.
- 95-100% – Describes me all, or almost all, of the time.

1. I have passion for my skating.
2. I am able to keep skating in perspective, especially in hard times.
3. I am dedicated to do everything I can to bring out my best each day.
4. I am mentally tough.
5. I thrive on challenges.
6. I have fun learning new things.
7. I am patient when learning or correcting things.
8. I enjoy pushing myself to my healthy limits.
9. I allow myself to be coached by showing up to lessons ready to focus, with an open mind, and with my body warmed up.

10. I communicate well with my team and/or partner (if appropriate).
11. I communicate well with my coach.
12. I communicate well with my parents.
13. I communicate well with the other members of my Inner Champion Circle.
14. I deal with problems as soon as they come up and ask for help from my Inner Champion Circle when I need it.
15. I am confident in my abilities.
16. I am an optimist.
17. I treat myself like I would treat my best friend.
18. I expect great – but realistic – things of myself each time I perform.
19. I keep focused on what I can control.
20. I stay in the moment.
21. I can easily deal with distractions.
22. I use mistakes as an opportunity to learn and get better.
23. I don't let setbacks stop me from getting what I want, because I know that setbacks are opportunities to learn and get tougher.
24. I practice with a purpose every day I skate.
25. I have a purpose during off-ice training.
26. I make every movement count when I am skating.
27. I know what I want to accomplish in each performance.
28. I am aware of my mind-body connection and can make adjustments to my mind or body when needed.
29. I skate for myself because it is my choice, and I don't rely on others for motivation.
30. I am disciplined, yet playful on the ice.
31. I use the power of my imagination, thoughts, and emotions to bring out my best each day.
32. I think it is just as important to be a good sport as it is to be a good athlete.
33. I enjoy sharing my love for skating with other people, judges included.
34. I understand that I may be a role model to other skaters, and I respect the responsibility that comes with being a role model.
35. I do a proper warm-up and cool-down every time I skate or train off ice.

36. I am on time for skating and off-ice training.
37. I get ready mentally and physically before I step on the ice to skate.
38. I take responsibility for myself, my practices, and my performances.
39. I am mentally flexible.
40. I am physically flexible.
41. I am able to deal with my emotions and moods so they don't affect my training.
42. I am aggressive and willing to take risks.
43. I am well conditioned and physically fit, and I listen to my body.
44. I practice how I want to perform so I can perform like I skate during practice.
45. I take time for other interests besides skating.
46. I respect myself, my team or partner (if appropriate), my coach, and others in my Inner Champion Circle.
47. I eat well and get enough sleep.
48. I take good care of my equipment, and I make sure I have everything I need each time I skate.
49. I am committed to my goals and to the goals of my team or partner (if appropriate).
50. I am committed to being an Inner Champion.

After you complete this exercise and get a well-rounded perspective of your Inner Champion qualities by using feedback from other people, celebrate your strengths and make a commitment to enhance the qualities that describe you less than 95% of the time. Next, create SMART and Positive goals that focus on making all fifty statements describe you at least 95% of the time. Finally, decide what actions you will take to achieve each goal.

Make a collage

Make a collage of inspirational sayings, quotes, pictures, and/or symbols. Use a variety of sources, such as magazines, newspapers, and websites. Hang your collage in your room above your bed or in a place where you will easily see it. Focus on your collage daily to help you stay in touch with your passion for skating and your commitment to bringing out your best. Update your collage or make a new one at least once a year for continuous motivation.

Show your appreciation

Give a boost to the passion your Inner Champion Circle has for your skating by showing your appreciation to all of the members. Send each person a card, an e-mail, or a picture with a note explaining how they help you, what they mean to you, and why you are thankful they are part of your Inner Champion Circle. If writing is not your style, express your appreciation by calling or telling them in person the next time you see them. Doing so will make their day and increase their motivation to continue giving you what you need from your Inner Champion Circle!

YOUR TIME TO SHINE HAS ARRIVED!

End Notes

Chapter 1
Bernard Ford. (July/August 1998). "Mental consistency in athletic preparation." *Professional Skater,* 12-13.

Chapter 2
Kristi Yamaguchi; from Lund, M. & Elfman, L. (July/August 1999). "A golden career." *International Figure Skating,* 64-65.

Linda Leaver; from Boitano, B. with Harper, S. (1997). *Boitano's Edge: Inside the Real World of Figure Skating.* New York: Simon & Schuster, p. 49.

Mission statement partially adapted from Ravizza, K. & Hanson, T. (1995). *Heads Up Baseball: Playing the Game One Pitch at a Time.* Indianaplois, IN: Masters Press.

Todd Sand; from Wessling, S. (1998). "True companions." *International Figure Skating,* 38-39.

Todd Eldredge. (January 2001). "Kids' questions." *Skating,* 68-69.

Johnny Weir; from staff report. (May/June 2004). "Short program: Proving his point." *International Figure Skating,* p. 16.

Audrey Weisiger. (January 2000). "Kids' questions." *Skating,* 68-70.

Brian Boitano; from Boitano, B. with Harper, S. (1997). *Boitano's Edge: Inside the Real World of Figure Skating.* New York: Simon & Schuster, p. 24.

Benjamin Agosto; from staff report. (May/June 2003). "Out of synch: Pairs and ice dance miss the beat." *International Figure Skater,* p. 53.

Skippy Baxter. (2004). personal conversation.

Barbara Roles-Williams. (May 28, 2004). PSA International Conference Presentation; San Diego, CA.

Frank Carroll; from Meyer, T. (September/October 1998). "Frank Carroll: 1998 coach of the year." *Professional Skater,* 20-21.

Robin Wagner. (Sept/Oct 2002). "2002 coach of the year: Robin Wagner." *Professional Skater Magazine,* 20-21.

Carole Yamaguchi; from Yamaguchi, K. with Ness, C. & Meacham, J. (1997). *Figure Skating for Dummies.* Foster City, CA: IDG Worldwide Books, p. 256.

Peter Carruthers. (January 2002). "Kids' questions." *Skating,* 66-67.

Chapter 3
Scott Hamilton. (May/June 1997). "Olympic champion Scott Hamilton diagnosed with testicular cancer." *Professional Skater,* p. 25.

Bernard Ford. (July/August 1998). "Mental consistency in athletic preparation." *Professional Skater,* 12-13.

Michael Weiss; from Leamy, E. (February 1999). "Father figure." *Skating,* 10-14.

Paul Wylie story adapted from Paul Wylie. (May 2002). US Figure Skating Governing Council Keynote Address; Minneapolis, MN.

Michelle Kwan. (February 6-8, 1998). "Olympic women: power & grace." *USA Weekend,* p. 7.

Brian Boitano story adapted from Boitano, B. with Harper, S. (1997). *Boitano's Edge: Inside the Real World of Figure Skating.* New York: Simon & Schuster, p. 87.

Sarah Hughes; from Elfman, L. (May/June 2002). "On top of the world." *International Figure Skating,* 34-37.

Kathy Casey. (2003). Kathy Casey Seminar motivational presentation; Santa Rosa, CA.

Elaine Zayak. (2003). personal conversation.

Ron Ludington; from Coulby, S. (December 1996). "Luddy." *Skating*, 25-27.

Tom Zakrajsek. (2004). PSA International Conference presentation; San Diego, CA.

B.L. Wylie. (May 2002). PSA International Conference presentation; Dallas, TX.

Chapter 4
Tara Lipinski; from staff report. (April 1998). "Tara reigns supreme." *Skating*, 11-15.

Paul Wylie. (January 2003). "Kids' questions." *Skating*, 78-80.

"Ribcage breathing" adapted from training sessions focused on "lateral rib breathing" with Sarah Johnson, M.A., Exercise Physiologist.

Muscular relaxation information adapted from Jacobson, E. (1930). *Progressive relaxation.* Chicago: University of Chicago Press.

Benjamin Agosto. (October 2001). "Kids' questions." *Skating*, 66-67.

Sasha Cohen. (September 2000). "Kids' questions." *Skating*, 54-55.

Carol Heiss Jenkins. (February 2001). "Kids' questions." *Skating*, 66-67.

Chapter 5
Brian Boitano; from Boitano, B. with Harper, S. (1997). *Boitano's Edge: Inside the Real World of Figure Skating.* New York: Simon & Schuster, p. 46.

Charlie Tickner. (2003). personal conversation.

Michelle Kwan. (2003). "Mindset of a Champion." ABC coverage of Skate America.

John Nicks. (2003). personal conversation.

Chapter 6
Haydenettes. (December 2002). "Kids' questions." *Skating,* 68-70.

Sasha Cohen; from Elfman, L. (September/October 2003). "Adventurous spirit." *International Figure Skater,* 54-55.

Naomi Lang and Peter Tchernyshev. (May, 1999). "Kids' questions." *Skating,* 50-51.

Jerod Swallow; from Miller, J. (April 1997). "Fresh faces: 1997 State Farm U.S. Championships." *Skating,* 12-18.

Tiffany Scott. (August/September 2000). "Kids' questions." *Skating,* 60-61.

Lynn Benson. (2004). personal conversation.

Peter Dunfield. (November/December 1998). "Giving a lesson." *Professional Skater,* 12-13.

Carole Yamaguchi; from Yamaguchi, K. with Ness, C. & Meacham, J. (1997). *Figure Skating for Dummies.* Foster City, CA: IDG Worldwide Books, p. 260.

Chapter 7
Scott Hamilton; from Fowler, B. (October 1997). "Healthy Hamilton to return to ice." *Skating,* p. 40.

Nancy Kerrigan; from USFSA. (1998). *The Official Book of Figure Skating.* New York: Simon & Schuster, p. 174.

Chapter 8
Nancy Kerrigan; from USFSA. (1998). *The Official Book of Figure Skating.* New York: Simon & Schuster, p. 174.

Chapter 9
Michelle Kwan; from Doren, K. & Jones, C. (2000). "Embrace your competitive spirit." *You Go Girl: Winning the Woman's Way.* Kansas City, MO: Andrews McMeel Publishing, p. 252. & Michelle Kwan; from Foster, S. & Prussack, T. (March/April 1999). "Learning to focus." *Skater's Edge,* 1-9.

Haydenettes. (December 2002). "Kids' questions." *Skating,* 68-70.

Kathy Casey. (2003). Kathy Casey Seminar motivational presentation, Santa Rosa, CA.

Timothy Goebel. (August/September 1999). "Kids' questions." *Skating,* 46-48.

Paul Wylie story adapted from Paul Wylie. (January 2003). "Kids' questions." *Skating,* 78-80.

Janet Lynn; from Hamilton, S. with Benet, L. (1999). *Landing It: My Life On and Off the Ice.* New York: Kensington Books, p. 52.

John Zimmerman; from Elfman, L. & Lund, M. (May/June 2002). "Center ice with the world." *International Figure Skating,* 38-41.

Elaine Zayak. (2003). personal conversation.

Christy Ness. (March/April 1999). "Consistency in skating." *Professional Skater,* 12-14.

Ken Shelley. (May 28, 2004). PSA International Conference Presentation; San Diego, CA.

JoJo Starbuck. (May 21, 1997). PSA International Conference Presentation, Nashville, TN.

Lynn Benson. (2004). personal conversation.

Ideas in the message to parents adapted from B.L. Wylie. (May 2002). PSA International Conference presentation; Dallas, TX.

Carole Yamaguchi; from Yamaguchi, K. with Ness, C. & Meacham, J. (1997). *Figure Skating for Dummies.* Foster City, CA: IDG Worldwide Books, p. 260.

Chapter 10
Peggy Fleming; from Doren, K. & Jones, C. (2000). "Find your passion." *You Go Girl: Winning the Woman's Way.* Kansas City, MO: Andrews McMeel Publishing, p. 7.

Tanith Belbin. (April, 2004). www.usfigureskating.org.

Debi Thomas; from Doren, K. & Jones, C. (2000). "Go for it." *You Go Girl: Winning the Woman's Way.* Kansas City, MO: Andrews McMeel Publishing, p. 66.

Timothy Goebel. (August/September 1999). "Kids' questions." *Skating,* 46-48.

Ken Shelley. (May 28, 2004). PSA International Conference Presentation; San Diego, CA.

Brian Boitano; from Boitano, B. with Harper, S. (1997). *Boitano's Edge: Inside the Real World of Figure Skating.* New York: Simon & Schuster, p. 121.

Peter Burrows; from Leamy, E. (August/September 1997). "A coach for life." *Skating,* 55-57.

Glossary

A

activation control. A mental skill that involves controlling your *activation level* by using *relaxation* and *energizing techniques*.

activation level. An individual's mental and physical energy level at a particular moment. Each person has an optimal level that is needed to perform at his or her best.

affirmations. Positive statements that are based on past successes, positive qualities, and desired goals.

attentional focus control. A mental skill that involves choosing where to focus one's attention, understanding how to deal with *distractions* in order to keep the appropriate focus, being able to have the appropriate focus for the required time, and knowing how to shift from one type of focus to another when necessary.

C

cue words. Words that direct one's mind and/or body to react in a certain way.

D

distraction. Anything that is not directly related to the task at hand, including negative thoughts and things not under a person's control.

E

energizing techniques. Methods that can be used to increase mental and physical *activation levels*.

energy zappers. Things that drain mental or physical energy.

enhanced healing. Refers to using mental skills in combination with physical rehabilitation to decrease the healing time of an injury.

events. Competitions, tests, exhibitions, critiques, paid performances, shows, etc.

external imagery. *Imagery* that is experienced from the external point of view, as if watching a video or observing from the audience. (See also *internal imagery*.)

extrinsic motivation. Motivation driven by external rewards, such as medals, fame, money, and placements.

G

goal setting. The act of planning what you want to accomplish by using the *SMART and Positive* guidelines.

I

imagery. Similar to a daydream, it is purposely initiated and can be controlled. Imagery can be used to mentally practice, prepare, and improve precision in skating and other endeavors. Sometimes called visualization and mental rehearsal. (See also *external imagery, internal imagery*.)

Inner Champion Circle. A skater's or team's support system. Members may consist of the parents or guardians of the skater(s), the coach(es), a sport psychologist, agents, sponsors, on- and off-ice trainers, significant others, and any other individual, professional, or organization – including school officials or an employer – contributing to the success of the skater or team.

internal imagery. Imagery experienced from the eye's point of view. (See also *external imagery*.)

intrinsic motivation. Motivation driven by internal rewards, such as pride, satisfaction, enjoyment, and feelings of accomplishment.

irrational thoughts. Thoughts that are not realistic or are not based on facts. These thoughts are often stated in extreme terms and include such words as **always** and **never**, or are in perfectionist terms that are impossible to attain.

M
mental rehearsal. See *imagery*.

mental skills. Skills such as *activation control, attentional focus control, goal setting, imagery, self-talk control,* emotional control, and time management, which can be learned and developed to increase the control a person has over reaching his or her potential.

mental toughness. The ability to control the *mind-body connection* in order to consistently be at one's best.

method of preparation for events. A carefully planned approach to mental and physical preparation for a specific event.

mind-body connection. The concept that the mind affects the body and the body affects the mind.

O
optimal performance. The best performance a person is physically and mentally capable of achieving.

P
periodization method of training. Varying intensity and type of on- and off-ice training throughout the skating season, designed to promote peaking at competitions and to avoid burnout and injuries.

plan of action after events. A consistent way to evaluate event preparation and performance.

plan of action during events. A pre-performance routine specifically planned to follow the day of an event. The routine involves both mental and physical components.

proprioception. The awareness of one's own body in space.

R
relaxation techniques. Methods to decrease mental and physical *activation levels*.

ribcage breathing. A breathing technique that involves inhaling through the nose deeply enough to fill one's ribcage area and exhaling through the mouth in a rhythmic matter.

S

self-confidence. A belief about one's true abilities that is based on facts and realistic expectations.

self-talk control. A mental skill that involves being aware of one's own internal dialogue, stopping any unwanted thoughts using a variety of techniques, and changing the unwanted thoughts to desirable thoughts.

SMART and Positive goals. Goals that are specific, measurable, action-oriented, realistic, time bound, and positive.

stressors. Things that cause mental or physical stress.

support team. See *Inner Champion Circle*.

T

team skater. A skater who is part of a pair, dance, synchronized, or theatre on ice team.

triggers. Words, images, or actions that direct the mind and/or body to react in a specific way.

V

visualization. See *imagery*.

Z

zone. Refers to the experience of the mind and body working together to produce an *optimal performance*.

Resources and Recommendations

Autobiography/Biography
Boitano, B. with Harper, S. (1997). *Boitano's Edge: Inside the Real World of Figure Skating.* New York: Simon & Schuster.

Fleming, P. (2000). *The Long Program: Skating Toward Life's Victories.* New York: Atria Books.

Hamill, D. (1983). *Dorothy Hamill On and Off the Ice.* New York: Alfred A. Knopf.

Hamilton, S. with Benet, L. (1999). *Landing It: My Life On and Off the Ice.* New York: Kensington Books.

Kwan, M. with James, L. (1997). *Heart of a Champion: An Autobiography.* New York: Scholastic Inc.

Lipinski, T. with Costello, E. (1997). *Triumph On Ice: An Autobiography.* New York: Bantam Books.

Torvill, J. & Dean, C. with Wilson, N. (1995). *Facing the Music.* Secaucus, N.J.: Carol Publishing Group.

Coaches & Parents
Lynch, J. (2001). *Creative Coaching.* Champaign, IL: Human Kinetics.

Martens, R. (1987). *Coaches Guide to Sport Psychology.* Champaign, IL: Human Kinetics.

Martens, R. (2004). *Successful Coaching.* Champaign, IL: Human Kinetics.

Orlick, T. (2002). *Feeling Great: Teaching Children to Excel at Living.* Ontario, Canada: Creative Bounds Inc.

Pipher, M. (1994). *Reviving Ophelia: Saving the Selves of Adolescent Girls.* New York: Ballantine Books.

Ryan, J. (2000). *Little Girls in Pretty Boxes: The Making and Breaking of Elite Gymnasts and Figure Skaters.* New York: Warner Books.

Silby, C. with Smith, S. (2000). *Games Girls Play: Understanding and Guiding Young Female Athletes.* New York: St. Martin's Press.

Thompson, J. (1995). *Positive Coaching: Building Character and Self-Esteem Through Sports.* Portola Valley, CA: Warde Publishers.

USFSA. (2002). *The Parents' Survival Guide: A Parent's Guide to Not Just Surviving the Skating Experience – But Enjoying It and Thriving in It!* Champaign, IL: Human Kinetics.

Wolf, R. (2000). *Coaching for Dummies.* Foster City, CA: IDG Worldwide Books.

Nutrition/Off-Ice Training/Sleep
Arbour, K. (2004). *The All New Ice Dynamics Injury Prevention and Conditioning.* www.icedynamics.net.

Clark, N. (2003). *Nancy Clark's Sports Nutrition Guidebook.* Champaign, IL: Leisure Press.

Jennings, D.S. & Steen, S.N. (1995). *Play Hard, Eat Right: A Parent's Guide to Sports Nutrition for Children.* Minneapolis, MN: Chronimed Publishing.

Lee, B. (2004). *Jump Rope Training: Techniques and Programs for Improved Fitness and Performance.* Champaign, IL: Human Kinetics.

Maas, J. (1999). *Power Sleep.* New York: Harper Collins.

Poe, C. (2002). *Conditioning for Figure Skating: Off-ice Techniques for On-ice Performance.* New York: McGraw-Hill.

Skating Books & C.D.
Mitchell, T. (2003). *Finding Greatness Within: Skating.* Philadelphia: Infinity Publishing. *Power Journal* is also available.

Mitchell, T. with Loundagin, C. (2000). *Sport and Soul: Skate for the Love.* www.innerchamp.com. Motivational audio C.D.

Shulman, C. (2001). *The Complete Book of Figure Skating.* Champaign, IL: Human Kinetics.

USFSA. (1998). *The Official Book of Figure Skating.* New York: Simon & Schuster.

Yamaguchi, K. with Ness, C. & Meacham, J. (1997). *Figure Skating for Dummies.* Foster City, CA: IDG Worldwide Books.

Skating Magazines
International Figure Skating. www.ifsmagazine.com

Recreational Ice Skating. www.skateisi.com

Skating. www.usfigureskating.org

The Professional Skater. www.skatepsa.com

Sport Psychology
Adrian, L.A. (1999). *The Most Important Thing I Know About the Spirit of Sport.* New York: William Morrow and Company.

Beals, K.A. (2004). *Disordered Eating Among Athletes: A Comprehensive Guide for Health Professionals.* Champaign, IL: Human Kinetics.

Clarkson, M. (1999). *Competitive Fire: Insights to Developing the Warrior Mentality of Sports Champions.* Champaign, IL: Human Kinetics.

Davis, G. (1999). *High Performance Thinking: For Business, Sports, and Life.* Colorado Springs, CO: Psychology Connections.

Doren, K. & Jones, C. (2000). *You Go Girl: Winning the Woman's Way.* Kansas City, MO: Andrews McMeel Publishing.

Heil, J. (1993). *Psychology of Sport Injury.* Champaign, IL: Human Kinetics Publishers.

Jackson, S.A. & Csikszentmihalyi, M. (1999). *Flow in Sports: The Keys to Optimal Experiences and Performances.* Champaign, IL: Human Kinetics.

Johnson, S. (2004). *Mind Wide Open: Your Brain and the Neuroscience of Everyday Life.* New York: Scribner.

Loehr, J. E. (1994). *The New Toughness Training for Sports.* New York: Plume.

Murphy, S., Editor (1995). *Sport Psychology Interventions.* Champaign, IL: Human Kinetics.

Nideffer, R. (1985). *Athletes' Guide to Mental Training.* Champaign, IL: Human Kinetics.

Nideffer, R. (1992). *Psyched to Win: How to Master Mental Skills to Improve Your Physical Performance.* Champaign, IL: Human Kinetics.

Orlick, T. (2000). *In Pursuit of Excellence: How to Win in Sport and Life Through Mental Training.* Champaign, IL: Leisure Press.

Ravizza, K. & Hanson, T. (1995). *Heads Up Baseball: Playing the Game One Pitch at a Time.* Indianapolis, IN: Masters Press.

Ravizza, K. (1992, 1993, 1994, 1995). Various lectures, symposiums, and workshops. Annual AAASP Conferences.

Silva, J. & Weinberg, R., Editors (1986). *Psychological Foundations of Sport.* Champaign, IL: Human Kinetics.

Walton, G. (1992). *Beyond Winning: The Timeless Wisdom of Great Philosopher Coaches.* Champaign, IL: Leisure Press.

Weinberg, R. & Gould, D. (2003) *Foundations of Sport & Exercise Psychology.* Champaign, IL: Human Kinetics.

Weinberg, R. (1988). *The Mental ADvantage: Developing Your Psychological Skills in Tennis.* Champaign, IL: Leisure Press.

Williams, J., Editor. (1986). *Applied Sport Psychology.* Palo Alto, CA: Mayfield.

Index

A

activation control 91-114
  events 176, 182
  injury 157-158, 161
  pain 166-167
  see energizing and relaxation
activation level 92-94
affirmations 67
  enhanced healing 157, 161
  events 45, 175, 180
  goals 44
  self-talk 79-80, 82
Agosto, Benjamin 48, 100, 198
attentional focus control 131-154
  changing focus 141
  control 133-134
  distractions 135
    techniques 136-139
  endurance 140
  enhanced healing 159, 161
  events 176-178, 182-183
  fatigue 134-135
  mistakes 139-140
  outside skating 143
  pain 168
  positive 132
  practice ice 177-178
  present 133
  self-talk 78

attentional focus control *continued*
  simple 134
  stress 134-135
  team skaters 142

B

bad habits 33, 68-69, 78
Baxter, Skippy 49
Belbin, Tanith 48, 100, 198
Benson, Lynn 131, 144, 189
body language 25-26, 80
Boitano, Brian 34, 46, 71-72, 115, 201
brain chemistry 24, 93-94
bribery 57
burnout 49-50, 53, 57-58, 155
Burrows, Peter 202

C

Carroll, Frank 52
Carruthers, Kitty 57
Carruthers, Peter 57
Casey, Kathy 79, 177
channeling energy 105, 122
Cohen, Sasha 102, 134
competition, *see events*
concentration 67, 132
confidence 33, 45, 46, 66-68, 76, 79-83
controlling effort 78
creating mood 78
cue words 78, 96-97, 104, 105

D

distractions 135
  techniques 136-139
Dulebohn, Philip 142
Dunfield, Peter 145

E

Eldredge, Todd 39
energizing 92-93, 103-106
  breaking it up 105-106
  breathing 104
  channeling energy 105
  cue words 105
  enhanced healing 158, 161
  environment 105
  events 176, 182
  imagery 104-105
  outside skating 106
  pain 166-167
  refocusing 105
energy zappers 92-93, 176
enhanced healing 155-164
  illness 155, 162
  injury prevention 155, 162
  mental skills 156-162
  mind-body connection 155-156
  resuming training 156, 160-161
  support 159-160
  team skaters 160
events 171-196
  checklist 178
  evaluation 183-185
  mistakes 173-174
  mock events 174-175
  on-ice warm-up 180-182

events *continued*
  plan of action during 178-183
  practice ice 177-178
  preparation 171-178
  pre-performance routine 178-179
external imagery 118-119

F

fatigue 78, 104, 134-135
fight or flight response 93-94
Fleming, Peggy 197
Ford, Bernard 19, 66
Ford, Henry 66

G

goals 31-64
  affirmations 44
  enhanced healing 156, 160
  evaluations 45-47, 184-185
  events 44-45, 175, 179-180
  imagery 44
  long-term 39
  outside skating 50
  setting 36-44
  short-term 39
  team 47-48
Goebel, Timothy 180, 199

H

Hamilton, Scott 65, 155
Haydenettes 131, 144, 173
Hughes, Sarah 53, 76

I

imagery 115-130
  details 117-119
  energizing 104-105

imagery *continued*
  enhanced healing 158, 161
  enhanced learning 120-121
  events 121-122, 176, 181, 182, 184
  external 118-119
  goals 44
  how it works 117-118
  improving elements 121
  internal 118-119
  muscle memory 116, 117
  outside skating 123
  pain 167
  practicing 119-120
  precision 121
  preparation 121-122
  relaxation 101-102
  self-talk 73-75
  team skaters 122-123
  timing 119
Ina, Kyoko 183
injury, *see enhanced healing*
Inner Champion Circle 41-44
  core members 42
  roles and responsibilities 42
internal imagery 118-119
irrational thoughts 76-77

J
Jenkins, Carol Heiss 107

K
Kerrigan, Nancy 162, 165
Kwan, Michelle 69, 122, 171

L
Lang, Naomi 135
Leaver, Linda 34
Lipinski, Tara 91
Ludington, Ron 83
Lynn, Janet 183

M
Meno, Jenni 37
mental practice 116
mental skills 21-27
mental toughness 19-30
  training journal 28
message to coaches 27, 50-54, 83-84, 106-108, 124-125, 143-146, 163, 169, 185-189, 201-202
message to parents 27, 54-58, 85, 108-109, 125, 147-148, 163, 169, 189-190, 201-202
mind-body connection 23-26
  enhanced healing 155-156
mission statement 34-35
  team 47
mistakes 133, 139-140, 142, 173-174
mock event 174-175
motivation 35, 49, 78, 105, 116, 141, 156, 158, 175, 197-198
muscular relaxation 97-100

N
Ness, Christy 186
Nicks, John 124, 187

O
off-ice training 155, 162
optimal performance 22

optimism 68-69, 75, 81, 142, 199

P

pain 165-169
  bad 165, 168
  good 165, 168
  mental skills 166-169
peak performance 22
perception 22-25, 67-69, 100
perfectionist 76-77
periodization, 155, 162
plan of action after events 183-185
plan of action during events 178-183
practice ice 177-178
practicing with a purpose 32, 33, 49, 172-173
Punsalan, Elizabeth 140

R

relaxation 91-103
  alert 94
  breathing techniques 94-97
  complete 94
  cue words 96-97
  distraction 102
  enhanced healing 157-158, 161
  events 176, 182
  imagery 101-102
  meditation 102-103
  muscular relaxation 97-100
  music 103

relaxation *continued*
  outside skating 106
  pain 166-167
  perception 100
  ribcage breathing 94-97
  stressors 92, 93
ribcage breathing 94-97
  energizing 104
  dealing with distractions 136-139
  relaxation 94-97
  self-talk 72
Roles-Williams, Barbara 51

S

Sand, Todd 37
Scott, Tiffany 142
self-confidence, *see confidence*
self-talk 65-90
self-talk control 67-90
  additional uses 77-78
  affirmations 79-80
  breathing 72
  confidence 66-68, 76, 79-83
  countering 72-73
  enhanced healing 157, 161
  events 175-176, 180-182
  imageries 73-75
  irrational thoughts 76-77
  outside skating 81-82
  pain 166
  perception 67-69
  thought stoppage 70-71
  time-out 73
  trigger 70-71

self-talk control *continued*
   unwanted thoughts 67-77
Shelley, Ken 187, 188, 200
SMART goal setting 36
   action-oriented 37-38
   measurable 36-37
   positive 39-40
   realistic 38
   specific 36
   time bound 38-39
Star Map 40
Starbuck, JoJo 187, 188, 200
stinking thinking 67-77
stress 92-103
stressors 92, 93
Swallow, Jerod 140

T

Tchernyshev, Peter 135
team cohesion 34, 47, 80
team skater 14
   affirmations 79-80
   attentional focus 142
   enhanced healing 160
   goals 47-48
   imageries 122-123
   mission statement 47
   self-talk 79-80

tests, *see events*
Thomas, Debi 198
thought stoppage 70-71
Tickner, Charlie 116
triggers 70-71

U

unwanted thoughts 67-77

V

visualization 116

W

Wagner, Robin 53
Weir, Johnny 42
Weisiger, Audrey 43
Weiss, Michael 68
Wylie, B.L. 85
Wylie, Paul 69, 94, 181

Y

Yamaguchi, Carole 55, 148, 190
Yamaguchi, Kristi 31

Z

Zakrajsek, Tom 84
zappers 92-93, 176
Zayak, Elaine 80, 184
Zimmerman, John 183
zone 22, 122, 162

About the author

Choeleen Loundagin, M.A. – The quest for athletic excellence has been Choeleen's passion throughout her life. A sport psychologist formally introduced her to the power of the mind-body connection and the benefits of using mental skills when she was a teenage competitive figure skater struggling with performance anxiety. His wisdom and the results it effected in her life inspired Choeleen to choose a career in the field of Sport Psychology. Now a respected performance enhancement consultant, Choeleen has helped athletes throughout the world bring more enjoyment to their sport experience and achieve their personal best. She consults with parents, coaches, and athletes in a wide variety of sports, at all levels of expertise.

Choeleen has a Master Degree in Sport Psychology, and her figure skating background as a competitor, U.S. Figure Skating triple gold medalist, international performer, and PSA Master Rated coach lends her special insight into the particular needs of skaters. In addition to her one-on-one consultations, Choeleen's *Mental Toughness Training Seminars for Figure Skaters, Parents, and Coaches* are in demand across the United States, and she is a frequent presenter at U.S. Figure Skating training camps and PSA seminars. A guest contributor to magazines such as *Skating, Professional Skater,* and *Recreational Ice Skating,* Choeleen is also co-producer of the motivational audio CD *Sport and Soul: Skate for the Love.*

Order Information

Order online: www.innerchamp.com

Postal orders: fill out form below and send with US funds to:

InnerChamp Books
PO Box 11362
Santa Rosa, CA 95406

Fund raising opportunities and group orders:
Contact 707-571-8023 or champion@innerchamp.com

POSTAL ORDER FORM

TITLE	*Price*	*Quantity*	*Total*
The Inner Champion Updated, second edition	*$24.95*		
Skate for the Love Audio CD	*$16.95*		
➔ **Order both and SAVE $$$** **The Inner Champion** & **Skate for the Love**	*$36.95*		
Sales tax (add 7.5% for orders shipped to CA):			
*Shipping: see prices below			
TOTAL ENCLOSED (US funds only)			

*Shipping: **Domestic:** $6.00 for 1-2 items; $3 each additional item
International: $10.00 for 1 item; $5 each additional item

Ship to:

NAME_____

ADDRESS_____

_____

PHONE_____ E-MAIL_____

More information on seminars, private consultations, and products

Mental Toughness Training Seminar for Figure Skaters, Mental Toughness Seminar for Parents and Coaches, & The Advanced Mental Toughness Seminar for Figure Skaters
Presented by Choeleen Loundagin, M.A.

At the skaters' seminar, athletes will learn first-hand from Choeleen. She'll bring to life the invaluable techniques from her *Inner Champion* book, plus answer questions about personal performance concerns. Written, verbal, and mental exercises will facilitate comprehension and retention of the material presented. The advanced seminar covers additional techniques designed to further strengthen the skaters' mental toughness.

The parent and coach seminars demonstrate effective methods for supporting the mental toughness training of skaters. Also covered: issues involving the skater/parent/coach triangle, motivational techniques, the application of sport psychology principles, philosophies of success, and how to ensure a positive sport experience. FMI: www.innerchamp.com

Private consultations with Choeleen Loundagin
Private consultations are available in person, by phone, or over the internet. An **invaluable resource** for advanced skaters, teams, coaches, those with highly personal issues, and anyone who wishes to further strengthen mental toughness and achieve full potential. FMI: www.innerchamp.com

Sport and Soul: Skate for the Love audio CD
Co-produced by Tom Mitchell, Ph.D., and Choeleen Loundagin, M.A.
This one-of-a-kind, highly effective performance enhancement tool contains an extraordinary compilation of sensational original songs, guided performance imagery, powerful affirmations, and motivational narrations – each designed to develop a winning attitude and bring out the best performances. A perfect resource for coaches teaching stroking and conditioning classes. FMI: www.innerchamp.com